IMAGES OF SPORT

OLDHAM RLFC

IMAGES OF SPORT

OLDHAM RLFC

BRIAN WALKER
OLDHAM RUGBY LEAGUE HERITAGE TRUST

TEMPUS

Left: Frederick Davies, a forward who joined Oldham from Newport Rugby Union Club in 1897. He is one of many Welshmen to have played for the club down the years.

Frontispiece: Oldham Rugby League Club has not just over the years produced many, many county and international players but has attracted players from each corner of the rugby-playing world. This painting by local artist Andy Pemberton is of the gathering of forty-two of those Oldham players, from various eras, from many countries; captains of Australia, New Zealand, Wales, England and Great Britain captured together in one frozen moment of time.
From left to right, back row: Maseesee Solomona, Bob Irving, Andy Goodway, Derek Turner, John Armstrong, Billy Farnsworth, Bryn Goldswain, Sid Little OBE, Bob Lindner, Hugh Waddell, Bob Sloman, Sir Phillip Sidney Stott, Ike Southward, Joseph Platt. Third row: Harry Varley, John 'Ben' Andrew, Syd Dean, Bert Avery, Bill McCutcheon, Bernard Ganley, Abe Ashworth, Alex Givvons, Ken Jackson, John Etty, Reg Farrar, A.E. 'George' Anlezark. Second row: Martin Murphy, Frank Stirrup, Mike Ford, Jim Lomas, George Tyson, Viv Farnsworth, Sid Rix, George (GW) Smith, Herman Hilton, Joe Ferguson. Front row: Alf Wood, Billy Hall, Terry Flanagan, George Frater, Arthur Lees, Alan Davies, Dave Holland.

First published 2005

Tempus Publishing Limited
The Mill, Brimscombe Port,
Stroud, Gloucestershire, GL5 2QG
www.tempus-publishing.com

British Library Cataloguing in Publication Data.
A catalogue record for this book is available from the British Library.

ISBN 0 7524 3466 7

Typesetting and origination by Tempus Publishing Limited.
Printed in Great Britain.

Contents

Left: Joe Ferguson. Oldham's greatest ever player. The Cumbrian forward joined the club in 1899 and between then and retirement in 1923 played in a record 627 matches for the Watersheddings side. He represented Cumberland, Lancashire, captained England and won 31 medals.

Acknowledgements

Many of the images featured in this publication come from the archives of the Oldham Rugby League Heritage Trust, but I would like to thank everyone who has provided photography, especially the *Oldham Evening Chronicle*. Thanks also to Geoff Cooke, Robert Gate, Mick Harrop, Michael Turner and Don Yates for their assistance in the compiling of the book.

A note on the Oldham Rugby League Heritage Trust:

In 1995 a group of Oldham's RL Club supporters first met to discuss those players to be inducted into the club's Hall of Fame. At that time it was realised that in and around the town there were a number of people who owned medals, representative caps, jerseys and other items of important memorabilia awarded to Oldham players from bygone eras and wished to donate them to the Hall of Fame. To protect the ownership of this ever-growing collection the trust was formed under the watchful eye of Oldham MBC Museum. By donation, short and long-term loan and purchase of items at auction the people of Oldham now have access to one of the best club rugby collections of artefacts in the world. The collection was recently displayed in the town's newly opened Gallery Oldham and during the four-week duration of the exhibition it received over 3,000 visitors and excellent reviews. A number of items from the collection are used by the author of this book to track the history of the Oldham club.

Introduction

During the Victorian era, rugby football evolved out of the public schools, through the universities, armed forces and civil service into the towns and cities of Britain. By the end of the 1870s it was being played not just by the upper classes but by large numbers of working-class men and boys throughout the United Kingdom and particularly in the industrialised areas of the North of England. The oldest rugby club in the country is Blackheath, founded in 1858, while the famous Manchester club started up in 1860 and the Rugby Union itself was formed in 1871. The first international – England *v.* Scotland – took place the same year, but five years on, in the early months of 1876, there was still neither club nor organised rugby played in Oldham.

This was soon to change when the Fletcher family and its three rugby-playing brothers arrived in town, having previously lived in Cheshire. One of the brothers, Abraham, had

played the game to a good standard with the Altrincham club and now wished to continue with the sport. The family became members of Werneth Congregational church, there gaining the ears of a number of local but influential businessmen and the political hierarchy, and the seeds for a rugby club in the town were soon sown. Oldham FC played its first match (remember it was fifteen-a-side rugby union) on a roped-off pitch on land known as Sugar Meadow in the Glodwick area of the town on 21 October 1876. Their opponents were Cheshire side Stalybridge, who narrowly won the game. And so it had begun. By 1879 forward John B. Rye had become the club's first representative player when he was selected to play for the Lancashire county side against Cheshire at Bowden and 128 years on, in 2004, Oldham's utility player Iain Marsh was representing Scotland in the European Nations Championship.

Sandwiched in between is a mixed history. On one hand there is the all-talented side that, between 1895 and the outbreak of the First World War, was never far away from the honours, the team that during the 1920s appeared in four consecutive Challenge Cup finals and the silky football provided by the Championship-winning side of the 1950s. On the other hand is the still hard-to-swallow pill that the side has not since won a major trophy for almost half a century, has never appeared at Wembley and in 1997 was forced to call in the receivers. The club, which just the season before it went into liquidation had played both in Super League and the World Club Championship in Australia, was quickly re-formed by a group of local enthusiasts, taking a place in the Second Division Championship for the opening of the 1998 season.

What follows is a pictorial snapshot of 128 years of rugby, both union and league, played by the famous Oldham club. In this book the Oldham side will often be referred to as the 'Roughyeds', a nickname associated with the club since Victorian times. It is a local term first recorded in 1834 by historian Edwin Butterworth referring to the ruffians who lived in the centre of town during the late eighteenth century.

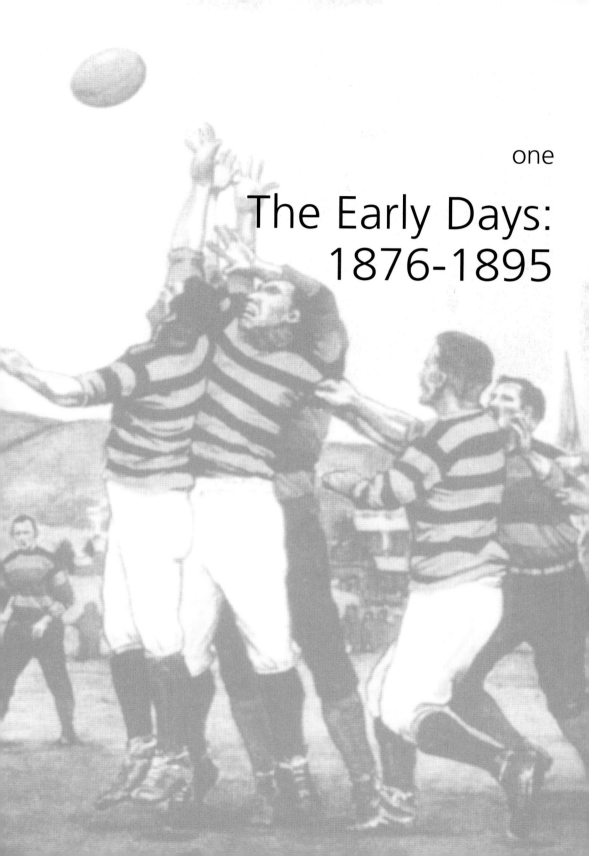

one

The Early Days:
1876-1895

Left: The Oldham club was founded in 1876 at a meeting held at the Prince Albert Hotel, Union Street West. Among those present were Abraham Fletcher, who had played rugby with the Altrincham club; William Chadwick, chairman of the town's Watch Committee (pictured); Fred Wild, a cotton-mill owner; Charles Hodgkinson, the chief constable of Oldham; and Alfred Emmott, who would eventually represent the town of Oldham in parliament.

Right: Club founder Alfred Emmott who, at a by-election in 1899, became Liberal MP for Oldham, beating off the challenge from the Conservative candidate Winston Churchill. At the General Election in 1900 he was re-elected, this time along with Churchill, who beat Emmott's fellow Oldham Liberal MP, Walter Runciman. Emmott represented Oldham at Westminster for eleven years, successfully fighting five elections, and in 1911 was elevated to the peerage.

Left: Club founder and Oldham's chief constable, Charles Hodgkinson.

Below: A painting depicting Oldham FC's first ever match against Stalybridge FC, played on a pitch adjacent to the then-recently rebuilt Glodwick Spinning Mill and known locally as Sugar Meadow. Oldham's original playing kit was black and amber hooped or striped shirts.

OLDHAM FOOTBALL CLUB.

FIRST TEAM.   SEASON 1877-8.

No. of Matches Played 28.   Won 12.   Drawn in favour 4.   Drawn against 1.   Lost 6.
Total Score:—Oldham, 16 Goals, 44 Tries, 58 Touchdowns, 30 Touches-in-Goal, &c.
Opponents, 4 „ 7 „ 23 „ 10 „

The earliest-known photograph of the Oldham team was taken during the 1877/78 season. Press coverage at the time was sketchy and if a match was covered at all by the local newspapers they devoted little more than a paragraph and only on the odd occasion did they mention any player by name, other than those who scored. The first time the team was named in the local press was during the club's second season. It was: T. Saville (full-back), J.K. Holroyd, W.G. Lloyd, J. Schofield (three-quarters), C. Doody, W. Chadwick (half-backs), A.M. Fletcher (captain), J.H. Mellor, J.H. Mallalieu, G. Travis, H. Fletcher, J.B. Cook, J.B. Rye, P.S. Stott, J. Fletcher (forwards). The fixture list for the club's second season included Wakefield Trinity, and Oldham were reputed to be the first Lancashire club side to play a match in Yorkshire.

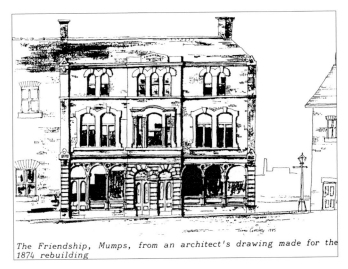

The Friendship, Mumps, from an architect's drawing made for the 1874 rebuilding

After just two seasons Oldham moved from Sugar Meadow to a fenced-off ground at Clarksfield vacated by Oldham Cricket Club. At the same time they made the Friendship Hotel, Mumps, their headquarters.

Oldham's early progress had been quite remarkable and now, in only their third season and the first at the new ground at Clarksfield, they lost only 2 of their 19 matches. John B. Rye became the first player to gain representative recognition when he was selected to play for Lancashire against Cheshire at Bowden, the first of 4 county appearances for the forward. Rye is the tall player, wearing his Lancashire shirt, fourth from left on the back row of this team photo taken five years later.

For no recorded reason, at the commencement of the 1880/81 season the steam train that was Oldham FC hit the buffers. By now several other clubs had been set up in and around the town, the two most prominent being Oldham Rangers and Oldham Juniors. It was to join these two clubs that Oldham FC players left in their droves and, to quote Alf Tetlow, an Oldham player at the time, 'It seemed that the Oldham club would disband owing to the difficulty in raising a team.' This was at a club that, just the season before, boasted three sides. It was thanks to the endeavours of official and player George Harrop (pictured here) that the day was saved when he persuaded Oldham Rangers and Oldham Juniors to join forces with the senior club. The name of Oldham FC survived and the 'new' club continued to play at Clarksfield.

In the midst of the turmoil of season 1880/81 the entrepreneurial Joseph Platt joined the club, although the reason why is not recorded but it was as an administrator that he was to make his mark. He was unassuming but forthright, determined and energetic, personal qualities that gained him respect and popularity. His business acumen eventually brought him directorships with various companies, but it was his position at the forefront of the forthcoming disputes with the Rugby Football Union for which Platt is best remembered. Based around arguments over broken-time payments, the dispute would culminate in 1895 with the breakaway of twenty-two Northern clubs to form the Northern Union. Platt would serve the new body in the capacity of secretary for twenty-four years, most of that time from his offices in Queen Street, Oldham. Platt would also serve the Oldham club as committeeman, treasurer and president until his death in 1930. History now shows that his work and efforts were fundamental in laying down the foundations of rugby league as we know it today.

The commemorative blue plaque unveiled in 1997 outside Platt's former offices in Oldham.

A member of the side during the 1880s was Philip Sidney Stott, in later life becoming club president and Sir Philip. This famous cotton-mill architect was responsible for designing mills all over Europe and India. In 1910 he ran for election as an Oldham MP, being beaten at the polls by Oldham FC founder Alfred Emmott. In 1929, living in Gloucestershire, he was awarded a baronetcy for his services to the Conservative Party.

Arguably one of the most famous Welshman ever to come north, the ex-Swansea three-quarter Bill McCutcheon made his debut against Manchester Rangers in 1888 and continued to play for the club until 1897. McCutcheon's greatest achievement was the winning of the Triple Crown when, in 1894, the Welsh RU side beat Scotland, England and Ireland. He was the only Oldham player ever to do so and one of only two Oldham players who played for Wales at union. When his playing career ended McCutcheon became a referee and club official, and by the time he retired had given thirty-eight years of continuous service.

The prestigious fixture against the first ever rugby touring side to this country, the New Zealand Native Football Team, better known as the Maoris, was played in March 1889. It was the highlight of the period during which the club played at Clarksfield and was one of the last matches before the move to Watersheddings. In order to help maximise the attendance, Oldham invited several guest players, including star backs Johnny Nolan and Bill Pennington from Rochdale Hornets, and Leigh's ace three-quarter Jack Hurst, helping the home side to narrowly beat the New Zealanders. The Maoris, excellent ambassadors of creed and country, played through a massive itinerary of 74 games, winning 49, losing 20 and drawing 5, going on to play a further 16 matches in Australia en route home.

THE RUGBY RUMPUS.

ALMONDBURY
GRAMMAR
SCHOOL
FOR
YOUTHS
OF
INDEPENDENT
MEANS
ONLY

PURITY
IN
FOOTBALL

THE REV. MASTER F——: Oh, fie, go away naughty boy, I shan't play with boys who can't afford to take a holiday for football any day they like!
MASTER M——LL——N: Yes, that's just you to a T; you'd make it so that no lad, whose father wasn't a millionaire, could play at the game at all in a really good team. For my part I see no reason why the men who make the money shouldn't have a share in the spending of it.

Little did anyone realise that the game against the Maoris, supported by a large gate-paying crowd, would turn the eye of Yorkshire rugby union zealot the Reverend Frank Marshall Oldham's way. Billed as 'the man with bell, book and candle facing the evil spirit of rugby professionalism', Marshall had already been instrumental in forcing some twenty investigations into professionalism involving clubs in his native county. This side of the Pennines Lancashire officials had been slower to react but, now encouraged by Marshall's success, they turned their attentions towards Oldham. However, they levied accusations that they could not back up and consequently were forced to drop. But the quality of player being assembled by the Oldham club didn't play for nothing and it wasn't over yet, not by a long chalk!

The twenty-one-year-old star three-quarter or full-back Jack Hurst joined Oldham from Leigh in time for the opening of the 1889/90 season, immediately forming a crowd-pleasing three-quarter partnership with Bill McCutcheon. A prolific try scorer, he would become one of the club's all time greats.

Watersheddings first opened its gates to the public at the beginning of the 1889/90 season. Swinton were the visitors, narrowly beating the home side in front of a 7,000 crowd. Oldham played for the first time in what was to become their trademark red and white hoops, replacing the bumblebee strip that they had been associated with for the last thirteen seasons. This painting depicts Swinton's famous England international three-quarter Jim Valentine beating Bill McCutcheon, before being cut off by the Oldham forwards.

Oldham's all-star side, brought together for the opening of the 1889/90 season. From left to right, back row: Darlington, Pendlebury, Giles, Joseph Platt (official), Holden, Fitton, Simpson. Middle row: S. Taylor (trainer), Armstrong, Bennett, McCutcheon (captain), Jack Hurst, Pennington, Harry Court (official and referee). Front row: Blomley, James Hurst, Thomas, Barnes, Gwynn, Nuttall.

Forward Edward 'Ned' Blomley became Oldham's ninth player to be selected for Lancashire, playing in the 1890 side against Cheshire at Birkenhead. His club caps have survived to this day. The version on the left (predominantly green) was presented to Oldham players up to around the year 1900, and was then superseded by a plum coloured one. This practice continued until around the early 1920s.

David Gwynn, the famous Welsh half-back, arrived at Oldham in 1890 from Swansea and under the residential rule qualified for Lancashire. During his first season in the North he played for his new county on 10 occasions, helping the team win the Championship. As a reward for their endeavours Lancashire were awarded a match against the Rest of England, both Gwynn and Bill McCutcheon representing the club. Before his arrival Gwynn had regularly played for his native Wales and continued to do so while at Watersheddings. The water jug and glass shown here are engraved with Gwynn's likeness and were presented to the talented half-back by the club in 1893, the season in which the team became Lancashire Champions and the last before his return to Wales. The inscription reads: 'DAVID GWYNN, CAPTAIN OLDHAM FOOTBALL CLUB, MARCH 11TH 1893'.

T. CRAVEN.   T. ROTHWELL.   J. BERRY.   W. McCUTCHEON.   J. PYKE.   T. KENT.   J. STRANG.
E. H. FLOWER.   T. WHITTAKER.   J. VALENTINE (Capt.).   W. ATKINSON.   T. MELLADEW.   T. COOP.
E. BULLOUGH.   D. GWYNN.   W. CROSS.   R. P. WILSON.

The Lancashire side that played England in Manchester in 1891. Oldham's Bill McCutcheon is fourth from the left on the top row and David Gwynn second from left, front row.

1896 — BRITISH TOUR OF SOUTH AFRICA
SECOND TEST at JOHANNESBURG

Back row: D. Cope, A. M. Beswick, J. H. Crosby, J. J. Wessels, T. A. Samuels, G. St. L. Devenish, P. Scott, W. S. Taberer.
Front row: J. B. Andrews, C. E. Devenish, A. Larard, E. T. D. Aston (Captain), H. H. Forbes, C. W. Smith, T. B. Mellet.

Ben Andrew (incorrectly captioned in the above picture as J.B. Andrews), the Oldham forward, was selected to play for Lancashire during the 1892/93 season but little did he realise that in less than four years time he would be playing for South Africa in the Second Test in Johannesburg against the British touring side. Seeking fame and fortune, he left behind the cotton mills of Oldham in favour of the gold fields of South Africa. He joined the Diggers RU club and represented both Transvaal and Johannesburg-Platterland against the British.

Left: Abe Ashworth, a forward with the local Werneth club and suspended *sine die* for professionalism, eventually had his suspension quashed and in 1891 rekindled his playing career by signing for Oldham. Ironically he would become the only Oldham player ever to represent England at union when, in 1892, he played against the Irish in Manchester. During his one season at Watersheddings he also played 5 matches for Lancashire before signing for Mossley and later Rochdale Hornets.

Abe Ashworth's representative caps. Left is his England cap, centre is his Lancashire county cap and to the right is the cap awarded for his participation in the North *v.* South trial for England.

Left: Baines' collectors card, probably issued to mark the arrival at Watersheddings of Abe Ashworth, a forward who, to quote a local news sheet of the period 'added steel to every pack of forwards in which he played'.

Below, left: The exciting young half-back Arthur Lees joined the Oldham side from the local Leesfield club in 1892. He eventually became club captain and played for Lancashire before and after the breakaway. Lees played three seasons for Oldham prior to the forming of the Northern Union in 1895, followed by a massive 356 matches under NU rules.

Below: Arthur Lees' Lancashire union shirt and Oldham cap, one of only a handful of pre-1895 county shirts that has managed to survive down the years.

ARTHUR LEES, the Lancashire County Half-Back,
Has Captained the Oldham Football Team through two remarkable seasons. What follower of the Oldham Team can ever forget that ever memorable match at Fallowfield, on the 29th of April, 1899, when Oldham became the "Champions of the Northern Union." This season, 1904-5, also under his Captainship, the Team have become the "Champions of the Northern League." Since the season 1895-96 he has scored for his Club 58 Tries and 3 Goals.

Above: 1893/94 Lancashire Club Championship medals awarded to Oldham players William Barnes and George Fillingham.

Right: Harry Varley, the England and Yorkshire half-back, was signed from the Liversedge club in 1893. He formed part of one of the best half-back partnerships that the club has ever had: Varley and Arthur Lees. Their exploits would become legend, the pair adding that extra dimension that would make a star-studded Oldham team into a trophy-winning one. The Lancashire Club Championship would be just the beginning of a run of success that would continue up to and after the First World War.

Opposite: Lancashire's big gate-taking clubs, Oldham included, put pressure on the county committee to come up with a more interesting and competitive set of fixtures than those negotiated between the clubs and as a result, the Lancashire Club Championship was introduced in 1892/93. The Watersheddings side won the trophy the following season and this cameo is of victorious club captain Bill McCutcheon surrounded by the 1893/94 squad.

FOR **BONSOR'S TESTIMONIAL.**

EMANUEL BONSOR was a successful and brilliant forward, and for 14 seasons played with the Oldham Rugby Football Club Teams, during which time he scored many tries. He was selected often to play for Lancashire County Team and he also toured with the County Palatine Team. He is the possessor of both the Rugby Union and Northern Rugby Union County jerseys. On two occasions his services have been appreciated by presentations purchased by public subscriptions. During his last season (1903—4) he Captained the "A" Team, with the result out of 27 matches they only lost one, and scored 569 points to their opponents 47 points.

Left: On 27 August 1895, as a result of a meeting held in Manchester, prominent Lancashire clubs including Oldham, knowing that there was never going to be any compromise shown by the Rugby Union in regard to the broken-time payment dispute, declared that they would fully support their Yorkshire colleagues in their proposal to form a Northern Union. Despite the heated politics Lancashire still continued to select a county side, the Oldham club providing a record eight players for matches held that season, four of them, three-quarter Ike Taylor, half-back Arthur Lees and forwards Ted Furniss and Emanuel Bonser making their debuts. Bonser, a local-born player, is featured in the photograph.

On the 29th of August 1895, two days after the Lancashire clubs made their decision to support their Yorkshire colleagues in their quest for the acceptance of broken-time payments, an historic meeting of twenty-one Northern clubs, Oldham included, took place at the George Hotel, Huddersfield, to debate their destiny. Twenty decided to vote in favour of a resolution to form the Northern Rugby Football Union and, joined by Cheshire sides Runcorn and Stockport, resigned from the RU. Oldham's Joseph Platt was appointed secretary.

two

Northern Union
Through to 1914

The period after the formation of the Northern Union in 1895 through to the First World War was truly a golden era in the history of the Oldham club. Never far away from the honours, it was a time of excitement and anticipation, from the day that Harry Varley led out his players onto the field at Hunslet for their very first match as members of the Northern Union on 14 September 1895, through to the middle of an Australian winter in 1914 when Roughyeds' stars Alf Wood, Billy Hall and Dave Holland helped Great Britain lift the Ashes in the famous 'Rorke's Drift Test'.

The club managed to lure to Watersheddings star players, not just from the length and breadth of Great Britain but from Australia and New Zealand too. Sid Deane, who would go on to captain Australia in the 'Rorke's Drift Test'; his fellow countrymen A.E. George Anlezark and Billy Farnsworth, who had played against the British tourists in 1910; Farnsworth's brother Viv, who toured here with the 1911 Kangaroos; the famous George Smith, vice-captain of the 1907 New Zealand All Golds; and English and Welsh rugby union internationals Tom Fletcher, Sam Irvin, Bill Nanson, Dave Holland, Alf Wood, Viv Huzzey and Jack Bedwellty Jones all wore Oldham colours.

The famous Cumbrian and Oldham forward Joe Ferguson led England to victory against the 1907 All Golds, while George Tyson, 'Mad' Arthur Smith, Bert Avery and Jimmy 'Jumbo' Lomas, for whom Oldham paid Salford a world-record transfer fee, all represented their country against the early Kangaroos.

The trophy cabinet was rarely empty. During its first six seasons in the NU, Oldham were twice winners and four times runners-up of the then-main competition for the Lancashire contingent, the Lancashire League. They became the first Lancashire side to lift the Challenge Cup when they beat Hunslet in the final of 1899. The Lancashire Cup, introduced in 1906, was brought back to Watersheddings on three occasions and seasons 1907/08 and 1909/10 saw Oldham top of the Northern Rugby League. This wonderful side was crowned Champions in 1909/10 and 1910/11.

Jack Hurst was the NU's leading try-scorer in the opening season of 1895/96, while winger Sam Williams was the sport's leading try-scorer for three consecutive seasons. The photograph is of Jim Lomas, the Great Britain captain for whom the club paid Salford a world-record transfer fee of £300 in 1911.

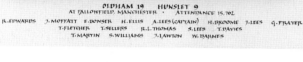

Right: Oldham were the first Lancashire side to lift the Challenge Cup when, in 1899, they beat Hunslet 19-9 in the final held at Fallowfield Stadium, the home of Manchester Athletic Club.

Above: The caps, badges and the 1899 Challenge Cup final jersey of Oldham's Welsh ace three-quarter Tom Davies. This is one of the finest surviving collections of representative and club caps from the Edwardian period.

Above, left: Lightening-fast Welshman Tom Davies, equally at home on the wing or in the centre, had played 14 times for Glamorganshire before signing for Oldham in 1898. Under the residency rule, he represented Lancashire and after leaving Watersheddings in 1901 to join Leeds also played for Yorkshire. The fleet-footed three-quarter quickly became a crowd-pleaser at Watersheddings scoring 60 tries from just 71 matches.

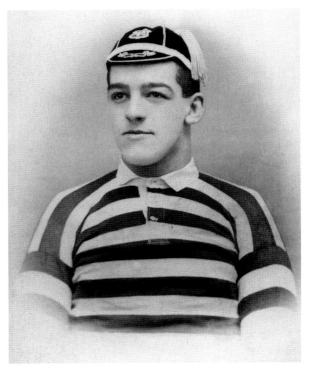

Herbert Ellis became a stalwart of the Oldham pack after joining the club in 1896 from Liversedge, where he had played an important role in establishing the Yorkshire club as County Champions. He played 234 matches for the Roughyeds, winning both a Challenge Cup winners' and Lancashire Championship medal. The tough-as-teak forward was one of only two players of that era who managed to win both the Yorkshire and Lancashire Championship.

Sam Williams, Oldham's brilliant winger, was the leading try-scorer in the Northern Union for three consecutive seasons at the turn of the nineteenth century. This hard-to-defend-against winger scored a total of 119 tries from 132 matches, and played for Lancashire on 8 occasions.

Right: Mercurial Cumbrian forward Joe Ferguson signed for Oldham after the 1899 Challenge Cup final and went on to play in a record 627 first-team matches, not retiring from the game until he reached the age of forty-four. Amazingly, he played through twenty-three seasons, won a massive thirty-one medals, played 16 matches for Lancashire, 31 for Cumberland and 4 for England. Without fear of argument Ferguson was the greatest Oldham player of all time and the first player to be selected when the club first considered its Hall of Fame.

Below: The 1899/1900 Lancashire side that beat Yorkshire 16-13 at Halifax included seven Oldham players: forward George Frater (top left); half-backs Arthur Lees (middle row, second left) and Joe Lawton (captain, holding the ball); three-quarters Sam Williams, Tom Davies and Tom Fletcher (fifth, sixth and seventh left, middle row); and full-back Dickie Thomas (far right, seated).

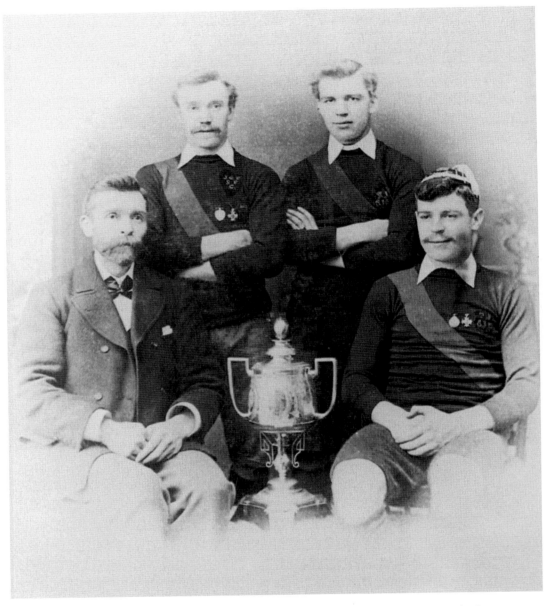

Tom Fletcher (sat on the right) joined Oldham having represented both Cumberland and England at union, being the first Cumberland back ever to be selected for his country when he played against Wales in Newport in 1897. This talented ball-handling three-quarter played 3 matches for Lancashire and 100 for Oldham, scoring 31 tries.

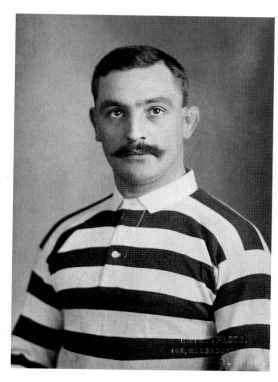

Left: Oldham-born George Tyson was one of the finest three-quarters ever to turn out for the club, scoring 111 tries from 246 first-team games between 1903 and 1911. He was the club's leading try scorer during three consecutive seasons and both played and scored tries in all three Tests against the first-ever Australian tourists, including the Ashes-deciding try in the closing minutes of the Third Test at Villa Park, Birmingham, in 1909. He was selected for the 1910 tour to Australia and New Zealand but declined for personal reasons.

Right: The first ever 'rugby league' international was played on Tuesday 5 April 1904 at Wigan's Central Park between England and Other Nationalities. Oldham provided forward Joe Ferguson and winger Frank Spottiswoode to the England team; Scottish forward George Frater captained the Other Nationalities, which also included two of Oldham's Welsh players, forward Dai Thomas and three-quarter David Lewis. Other Nationalities won the match 9-3. The photograph is of winger Frank Spottiswoode, who joined the Watersheddings side in 1901 from Carlisle RU.

The photo is of the 1904/05 Oldham team that won 25 and drew one of its 34 league matches to win the Championship. From left to right, back row: H. Topham, D. Thomas, A. Jardine, H. Ellis, A. Lees (captain), J. Vowles, G. Frater, J. Wright, A. Glossop (trainer). Middle row: T. White, J. Wilkinson, T. Sellers, G. Tyson, C. Civil, S. Lees, J. Owens, R. Carpenter. Front row: R.L. Thomas, F. Spottiswoode, T. Cash, D.J. Lewis, T. McLean, J.R. Lawton.

Three of the medals awarded to the 1904/05 Championship-winning squad presented to James Kelley, Billy Dixon and Dai Thomas.

Right: Forward 'Mad' Arthur Smith joined the club during the 1905/06 season from the West Country union side Yorkley and Cinderford. One of the star packmen of the multi-talented Oldham team of the pre-First World War era, Smith, whose nickname was awarded because of his 'forceful' style of play, was selected 6 times for both England and Great Britain and played 247 first-team matches for Oldham, before joining Halifax just before the outbreak of war.

Left: Half-back Tom White was a masterpiece of a signing. This talented player, who joined the Roughyeds in 1905 from the Bath union club, had previously been reserve for the English union side and could turn his hand to playing anywhere in the backs. He captained the Watersheddings side, played 224 first-team matches scoring 49 tries and kicking 81 goals, as well as playing 5 times for England and once for Great Britain. White ended his career with the Coventry rugby league side, which he joined in 1913.

Oldham beat the 1907/08 New Zealanders, the first national side to tour the Northern Union, 8-7 at Watersheddings. Joe Ferguson and Arthur Smith played in the England pack that beat the Kiwis at Wigan, while Tom Llewellyn, Arthur Smith, George Tyson and Tom White represented Great Britain in the Test Series won 2-1 by the Kiwis. The tourist's vice-captain and three-quarter George Smith was persuaded to sign for Oldham at the end of the tour. The former All Black was talented at many sports and is a member of the coveted New Zealand Sports Hall of Fame. Acclaimed as 'probably the most versatile sportsman ever produced by New Zealand', an accomplished rugby player, champion jockey and world-record holder for the 440-yard hurdles, he appeared in 173 first-team games for the Roughyeds. The G.W. Smith medal is now awarded to the Man of the Series in each Great Britain v. New Zealand Test Series. Smith is on the left-hand side of the two players sat on the front row of this informal team photograph of the 1905 All Blacks.

While season 1907/08 would go down in rugby league history as the great Hunslet club's four-cup-winning season, Oldham topped both the Northern Union (Hunslet were second), the Lancashire League and also won the Lancashire Cup.

Right: In 1909 Oldham beat the first-ever Australian touring side to this country 11-5 and also had winger George Tyson, forwards Arthur Smith and Billy Longworth selected for each of the three Tests. The First Test held in London was drawn 22-22, the second, played at Newcastle-upon-Tyne, was won 15-5 by Great Britain and the final Test, played in Birmingham, was won 6-5 by the Lions to take the Ashes.

Above, right & left: At the end of the 1908/09 tour, three of the Kangaroos signed for Oldham; three-quarter or half-back Sid Deane from Norths, who would progress to captain Australia (there is a photograph of Deane on page 46 of this book), half-back George Anlezark (left) from the North River club, and forward Tom McCabe (above) from the Glebe club but who was originally born in Widnes.

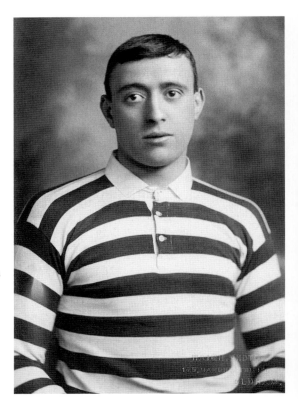

Right: Locally born forward Billy Longworth made his Oldham debut in 1904, the first of 146 matches before signing for Halifax in 1912. This tall, clever ball-player was an ideal candidate for the loose-forward position, a vital role after teams were reduced from fifteen to thirteen players for the 1906/07 season. He played twice for Great Britain, 4 games for England and 5 for Lancashire.

J. MILLER.

Left: James Miller holds the Oldham record for tries in a match, the winger scoring 7 against Welsh side Barry in 1908.

Left: Twenty-seven-year-old forward William Moore Bell Nanson, who had played twice for the England RU side, linked up with former playing colleague Frank Spottiswoode when he joined the Roughyeds from Carlisle RU in 1908. He played only 28 first-team matches before joining Coventry two years later. Nanson was killed in action at Gallipoli during the First World War while serving with the Manchester Regiment and was posthumously awarded the Queen and King's Medal for Gallantry.

Below: Season 1909/10 saw the Roughyeds top of the league, winning 29 and drawing 2 of their 34 league matches. They also won the Lancashire League and became Champions when they beat Wigan 12-7 in front of a crowd of 10,850 on Broughton's Wheater's Field ground. George Smith, Billy Dixon and Tom McCabe scored the tries while Alf Wood and Joe Ferguson kicked a goal each. From left to right, back row: G.W. Smith, Avery, Jardine, A. Smith, Helm, Wood, Tyson. Front row: White, Cook, Llewellyn, Ferguson, Anlezark, Owens. Inset: Deane.

Photo by R. Scott & Co.   **OLDHAM R.F.C.**   *Manchester.*

G. W. Smith,   A. Avery.   Jardine   A. Smith,   Helm,   Wood.   G. Tyson,

Inset—S. Dean   T. White   Cook   Llewellyn   Ferguson   Anlezark   Owens

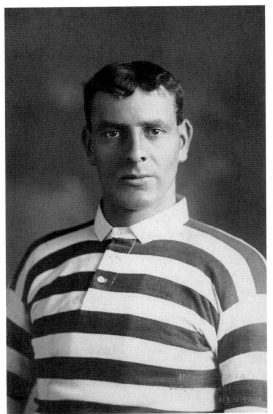

Above: Bert Avery, signed from Devonport Albion RU in 1905, played 289 matches for the Oldham first team as well as 6 for Lancashire, 5 for England and 4 for Great Britain. Along with fellow club forward Tom Helm, he was selected for the first ever Australasian tour in 1910, during which he played in the first two Tests against the Kangaroos. Both were won to retain the Ashes. Famous for his rampaging runs, helped along by a determined hand-off, this big, fast, ball-playing forward was one of the finest players to pull on the red and white jersey. This unusual photograph of Avery sees him posing in front of the crowd.

Left: Scottish forward Tom Helm signed for Oldham from the Hawick union club in 1909. He was selected for the 1910 tour to Australia and New Zealand but became ill on the outward journey and took no active part in any of the matches. Helm played just 43 first-team matches for the Roughyeds before leaving Watersheddings at the end of the 1910/11 season.

Tom Helm's 1910 tour cap can be seen displayed in Hawick Museum.

Oldham broke the bank when, in 1911, they paid Salford a then world record transfer fee of £300 for the signature of the skilful but powerful three-quarter James 'Jumbo' Lomas. The Watersheddings management saw the captain of the 1910 tour side as the key to retaining the Championship, and they were duly rewarded when he scored 13 tries during the last 17 matches of the season. While at Watersheddings he represented Great Britain twice, England 3 times and also played for his native Cumberland on 3 occasions before being transferred to York in 1913. The painting of the 1911 Oldham *v.* Runcorn match by artist Steve Bennett highlights Lomas passing the ball.

PRIVY PURSE OFFICE
BUCKINGHAM PALACE

8th April, 1911.

My dear Derby,

In reply to your letter of the 3rd inst.,

I have to say that The King is graciously pleased to become

Patron of the Northern Rugby Football Union.

Yours sincerely,

W. H. P. Carington

The
Earl of Derby, G.C.V.O.
&c., &c., &c.,

Joseph Platt, tired of the prejudices continuously aimed in the direction of the Northern Union and doggedly determined to raise the profile of the sport, persuaded the Earl of Derby to accept its presidency and in turn used the Earl to persuade George V to become patron. Remarkably, a long-forgotten series of letters negotiating and finally confirming acceptance of these positions were discovered a few years ago in a discarded shoebox in an Oldham attic.

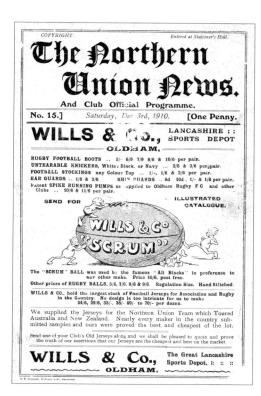

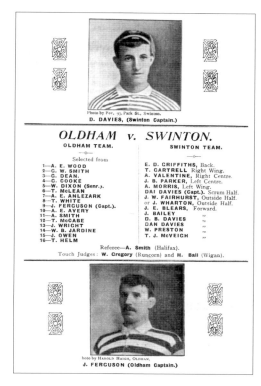

Broughton's Wheater's Field was again a lucky ground for the Oldham side during seasons 1910/11 and 1911/12. They beat Swinton 4–3 in the 1910 Lancashire Cup final and in the last match of the campaign beat Wigan 20-7 in the final of the Championship. The following season they retained the Lancashire Cup there, beating Rochdale Hornets 12-5 and then Wakefield Trinity 17-0 in the semi-final of the Challenge Cup. Unfortunately, the final of the Challenge Cup, held at Headingley, was lost 8-5 to Dewsbury.

Oldham beat the 1911/12 Kangaroos 14–8 at Watersheddings and, by the end of the Ashes–winning tour, Australian brothers Viv and Billy Farnsworth had signed for the club. The siblings had together played for Australian club side Newtown and could both play either at centre or half-back. Viv played 78 matches for Oldham before leaving the town at the outbreak of war in 1914, but Billy continued to represent the club until midway through the 1919/20 season, playing in 93 matches. The photograph is of Viv Farnsworth.

Right: Evan Davies had recently played in the Welsh union trials when the brilliant Llanelli three-quarter was persuaded to move north in 1911 and sign for the Roughyeds. One of the great centres who played for Oldham, he would play a massive 321 matches in the first team, scoring 102 tries and, while the war interrupted his career, he played 3 times for both his native Wales and Great Britain and was also selected for the 1920 tour to Australia.

Below: Oldham overcame Broughton, Widnes and St Helens before beating Wigan 5-0 in the 1913/14 Lancashire Cup final. The photograph is of the medal presented to Oldham forward Joe Ferguson.

Full-back Alf Wood, centre Billy Hall and forward Dave Holland were the three Roughyeds selected for the 1914 tour to Australia, all three playing a role in the most famous rugby league international of all time, the 'Rorke's Drift Test', an Ashes decider played on Sydney Cricket Ground. Without notice, the Australians amended the tour schedule so that all three Tests were played within a week and, despite protesting and being without the services of at least six Test regulars, Harold Wagstaff's Lions beat off the challenge of the Kangaroos to win the Third Test 14–6. Oldham's Billy Hall was concussed ten minutes from time, becoming the third player forced to leave the field for the Lions and, just before the end, the side was down to nine players when Halifax's W.S. Prosser was badly winded. The remaining nine managed gallantly to protect their lead to clinch the series. Oldham's full-back Alf Wood, who had bravely started the match with a broken nose, scored 8 of the Lions' 14 points, kicking 4 goals.

This painting is of the Oldham trio helping to tackle Australian winger Dan Frawley. The Lions in those days played in red and white hooped shirts and the Kangaroos in maroon and blue.

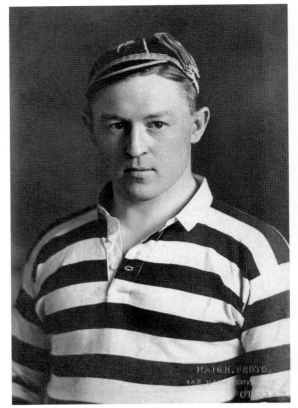

Right: Wolverhampton-born Alf Wood had played union for county sides Devonshire and Gloucestershire and 3 times for England before signing for Oldham in 1908. The full-back played 244 matches for the Roughyeds where he won every honour in the game with the exception of a Challenge Cup winners' medal. Wood, who played 4 matches for Great Britain and 2 for England as a league player, toured in both 1914 and 1920 when, at the age of thirty-six, he was the oldest player ever to do so. He also played soccer for Oldham Athletic.

Below: Alf Wood's England RU international and 1920 tour caps. The England cap was recently unearthed in Oldham and his 1920 tour cap rediscovered in Kirkcaldy.

D Hollands
Devenport Albion &
Oldham F.C.

Left: Forward Dave Holland was a member of the Gloucestershire union side that won the County Championship in season 1909/10 and played in the 1912 England union side. He signed for Oldham in 1913 from the Plymouth-based Devonport RU club, where he had also represented Devonshire. When selected for the 1914 tour he played in each of the three Tests against Australia and against New Zealand in Auckland. His last first-team match for Oldham was against Leeds at Headingley in 1921.

Below: Two of international forward Dave Holland's medals, won while playing for Oldham. On the left is his 1913/14 Lancashire Cup winners' medal and on the right is his 1922/23 Northern Combination winners' medal, which was won while playing second-team rugby towards the end of his career. The medals were discovered wrapped in a newspaper, which included a copy of his obituary, in a house in Gloucester in 2001.

Above: The youngest of seven brothers, William 'Billy' Hall, like his six siblings before him, played union for Gloucestershire and in 1912 was also selected to play union for an England XV against France. He started his career with Oldham in 1913 as an elusive centre or stand-off who quickly established himself in league, culminating in his selection for the 1914 tour, during which he played in all three Tests against the Kangaroos. He played in the Oldham first team until 1925, scoring 53 tries from 240 matches.

Right: Australian back Sid Deane signed for Oldham at the end of the 1908/09 tour to Great Britain, playing 103 first-team matches before returning to Australia in 1914 in time to captain the Kangaroos in the three Test matches against the Lions.

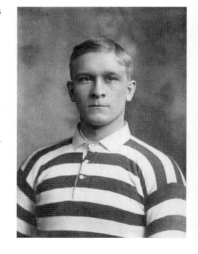

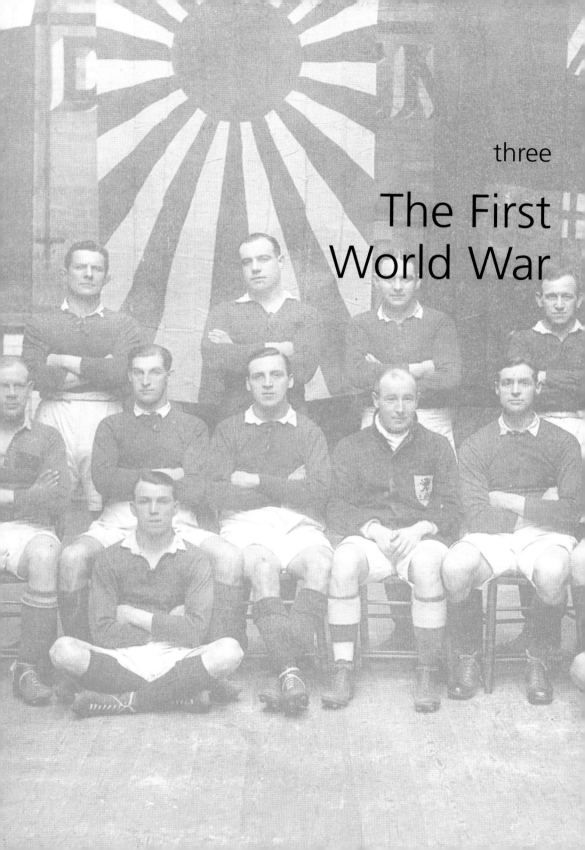

three

The First World War

PLAYING THE GAME.

Oldham N.U. players, like many others, have "gone for the line."

Statistics indicate that Oldham provided more of its players, officials and staff to the war effort than any other Northern Union club. During the first two years of the First World War the club played only friendly matches, but most weekends the club found it difficult to raise a team and closed down for the duration in 1917.

At the end of hostilities the club mourned the death of many of its young supporters and seven of its playing staff. Of the forty-eight Oldham players who had served in the war Arthur Smith, Tommy Cash, William Biggs and J. Swithenbank all won the Military Medal, while Fred Wise was awarded the Distinguished Conduct Medal. Club officials John Rye and W. Patterson both achieved the rank of lieutenant-colonel.

The poignant photograph is of the Royal Navy Depot union team, taken early on in the First World War, and features Oldham's forward Dave Holland (second left on the back row).

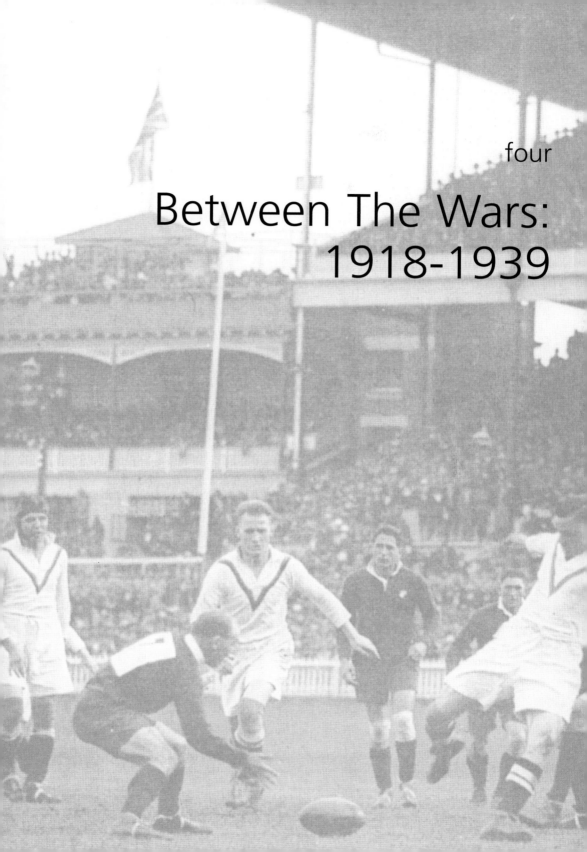

four

Between The Wars: 1918-1939

Until broken by the great Wigan side of the 1990s, Oldham held the proud record of being the only club to appear in four consecutive Challenge Cup finals (albeit before the match was taken to Wembley). The run started in 1924 when they lost 21-4 to Wigan at Rochdale's Athletic Grounds, followed in 1925 by a 16-3 victory over Hull KR at Headingley. Then, in 1926, they lost 9-3 to Swinton back at the Athletic Grounds and finally took revenge on the Lions by beating them 26-7 in the 1927 final played at Central Park. While not possessing quite as much flair as the pre-First World War side, the team certainly knew how to do well in the cup competitions and besides reaching those four consecutive Challenge Cup finals they reached the final of the Lancashire Cup in 1918, 1919, 1921, 1924 and 1933, winning the trophy three times. Add to that the honour of being top of the league table at the end of 1921/22 and being Lancashire League Champions in 1922, and the period between the wars was certainly rich and rewarding for both club and supporters.

On the representative front Oldham provided three players for the 1920 tour, forward Herman Hilton, three-quarter Evan Davies and seasoned full-back Alf Wood. Forwards Bob Sloman and Albert Brough and backs Sid Rix and Ernest Knapman were the club's four representatives on the 1924 tour and, while Bob Sloman was the only Oldham player to be selected in 1928, the joint-tour manager was club official George Hutchins, who was re-elected to the same position in 1932. Jack Oster and Tommy Rees also represented Great Britain; Rod Marlor, Tom Holliday, Bill Hall, Bob Sloman and Edgar Brooks all played for England, as did Alf Higgs, Joe Corsi, Reg Hathway, Fred Brown, Ambrose Baker, Trevor Thomas, Ned Thomas, Alex Givvons, Norman Pugh and Lewis Rees for Wales. Irishman Bill Kirkpatrick and Welshmen Ambrose Baker and Emlyn Watkins were picked to represent the Other Nationalities and Oldham's Australian three-quarter Graham Macrae played for a Dominions XIII.

The photograph is of the 1919 Lancashire Cup winning side. From left to right, back row: F. Pearce, G.F. Hutchins, J. Blunn, A. Anlezark, A. Lees, T. Potter, W.H. Greaves, J.W. Wroe, J. Taylor, A.E. Tetlow. Third row: J. Wild, J. Oakes, A.J. Swann, R. Wylie, J. Collins, W. Biggs, W. Thomas, A. Moore, P. Carter, E. Davies, C. Hutchins, J. Finnerty, H. Langton, F. Howarth. Second row: A. Harrop, H. Hilton, W. Hall, J. Ferguson, G.W. Holden, D. Holland, J. Parkinson, T. Fitton, R. Thompson. Front row: D. Thompson, M. Tighe.

Left: Local-born Herman Hilton was one of the greatest forwards ever to play for Oldham. Signed from Healey Street amateur side, Hilton made his debut for the Roughyeds in 1913 and went on to make 253 appearances during a war-interrupted career, the last in 1925. Hilton was arguably the star forward of the 1920 Lions' tour, playing in each of the three Tests against both the Kangaroos and the Kiwis, scoring 2 tries in the 23-13 victory against Australia in Sydney. Having lost the Ashes, the Lions were looking for revenge when Australia visited Great Britain the following year. Herman Hilton helped ensure this would be the case, scoring a try in the decider held at Salford, the Lions winning a bruising encounter 6-0. Hilton's representative honours included playing twice for Lancashire, 7 times for Great Britain and 3 for England.

Right: Herman Hilton played in the first two of Oldham's four consecutive Challenge Cup final appearances, captaining the side to a 16-3 victory against Hull KR at Headingley in 1925. The painting 'Local Heroes' depicts Hilton holding the Challenge Cup aloft.

Left: Herman Hilton's representative caps and Lancashire jersey badge. From left to right: England cap, Lancashire county cap and 1920 tour cap.

51

Left: Rothwell (Rod) Marlor signed for the Roughyeds from local amateur side Salem Hornets in 1914. A rugged prop-forward with an uncompromising style of play, he played twice for England, three times for Lancashire and 264 times for Oldham, including three Challenge Cup finals. His last league appearance in an Oldham jersey was against Pontypridd in 1927.

Below: This painting is of Oldham's left-wing speedster and record try-scorer Reg Farrar warding off Huddersfield's skipper Len Bowkett in a match played at Watersheddings in 1929. Signed from the Halifax Old Boys union club, the free-scoring Farrar soon became a favourite with the Oldham supporters. He scored a try and 2 goals in the 1925 Challenge Cup final victory against Hull KR and from his 143 first-team outings scored 114 tries. His 49 touchdowns in 1921/22 is still a club record and while at Watersheddings he won a Yorkshire county cap.

Right: Ernest Knapman was one of many players that Oldham sourced from the West Country. The Devonshire union county full-back, born in Torquay, signed for the club in 1921 and played in the 1924, 1925 and 1926 Challenge Cup finals as well as a further 203 first-team matches. Selected for the 1924 tour, he played against New Zealand in Auckland, his only other representative appearance being for England against Wales at Workington in 1925.

Below: Taking a casual pose inside the Oldham pavilion are the four Oldham players selected for the 1924 tour. Left to right are giant forward Bob Sloman, full-back Ernest Knapman, forward Albert Brough and three-quarter Sid Rix. Great Britain won the Ashes series 2-1, Rix playing in all three matches and Brough in the second, which proved to be the decider. New Zealand won a three-match series by two Tests to one, Rix playing in all three, Knapman in the second and Brough in the third, the only victory. Sloman suffered a bad injury during the early part of the tour and took no part in any of the Tests.

Left: Albert Brough (seen here watching over the tackle in a match against Batley in 1926) signed for the Roughyeds in 1923 from Barrow. This speedy back-row forward, who could turn his hand to playing in the backs, was also an excellent kicker, topping the club's goal-kicking charts through four consecutive seasons. He played in all four of Oldham's Challenge Cup finals of the period, twice for Great Britain and 6 times for Lancashire.

Right: Towering forward Bob Sloman, signed from the Plymouth Albion union side in 1921, would serve Oldham for eight seasons including a period as captain. The long-striding, speedy forward was one of only two Oldham players selected for consecutive tours to Australia and New Zealand. He played 268 matches for the Roughyeds, scoring 40 tries, and 5 times for both England and Great Britain. He was the last Oldham captain ever to hold aloft the Challenge Cup when the side beat Swinton 26-7 in the final at Wigan in 1927.

Left: Three-quarter Sid Rix, born in Irlam, joined Oldham at the end of the First World War. He could play equally well either on the wing or in the centre, is second only to Alan Davies in the Oldham all-time try-scoring list and is rightly recognised as one of the best three-quarters ever to play for the Roughyeds. He played in all six Test Matches on the 1924 tour and in three against New Zealand when they toured here during 1926/27, as well as playing 6 games for Lancashire.

Oldham 3 St Helens Recreation 3. Watersheddings action from 1926.

The 1925, 1926 and 1927 Challenge Cup final programmes.

In 1926 club official George Frederick Hutchins was selected to be Oldham's representative on the rugby league council, an important step to becoming one of the sport's greatest administrators. Joint-manager of both the 1928 and 1932 tours (the Ashes were won on each occasion), pioneer of the sport in France and schoolboy rugby in Oldham, he was honoured by having the famous two-tiered stand at Watersheddings named after him.

Right: Jack Read had played union 5 times for Gloucestershire before signing for Oldham from the Gloucester club itself in 1926. One of the finest props to have served the club, Read played a massive 463 matches (second only to Joe Ferguson), his career spanning fourteen seasons. He played in the Challenge Cup finals of 1926 and 1927, and the Lancashire Cup final of 1933 when the Roughyeds beat St Helens Recreation 12-0 at Swinton.

V SCOTLAND, EDINBURGH 17·3·1923
A·T·VOYCE H·H·LOCKE G·S·CONWAY R·COVE-SMITH E·MYERS A·M·SMALLWOOD
W·G·E·LUDDINGTON A·F·BLAKISTON C·N·LOWE W·J·A·DAVIES(c) W·W·WAKEFIELD C·R·KERSHAW
F·W·SANDERS
E·R·GARDNER T·H·VILE (REF WRU) T·E·HOLLIDAY

Tom Holliday was the captain who led the joint counties of Cumberland and Westmorland to the heady heights of being 1924 English RU County Champions. He played 7 times for the England union side and toured South Africa in 1924 but, owing to the 1920s Depression and the massive unemployment that went with it, the classy back joined the professional ranks at Oldham. Signing in 1926, he won a Challenge Cup winners' medal in his first season and during his relatively short stay with the club Holliday made 83 appearances, scoring 33 tries, while he also played 7 times for his native Cumberland and once for England. For sixty-nine years Holliday held the record for being the last player to score a hat-trick of tries in a Challenge Cup final. He starred as a full-back in union but it was on the wing that he made his mark with Oldham. Holliday is pictured here (sat on the right of the front row) in the England union side that beat Scotland in Edinburgh in 1923.

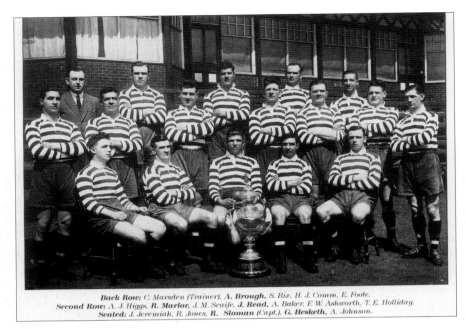

Back Row: C. Marsden (Trainer), **A. Brough**, S. Rix, H. J. Comm, E. Foote.
Second Row: A. J. Higgs, **R. Marlor**, J. M. Scaife, **J. Read**, A. Baker, F. W. Ashworth, T. E. Holliday.
Seated: J. Jeremiah, R. Jones, **R. Sloman** (Capt.), **G. Hesketh**, A. Johnson.

The Oldham squad that beat Swinton 26-7 in the 1927 Challenge Cup final. The match, played on Wigan's Central Park ground, was watched by a massive 33,448 crowd and would be the last time that the Roughyeds lifted the cup. From left to right, back row: C. Marsden (trainer), A. Brough, S. Rix, H.J. Comm, E. Foote. Second row: A.J. Higgs, R. Marlor, J.M. Scaife, J. Read, A. Baker, F.W. Ashworth, T.E. Holliday. Seated: J. Jeremiah, R. Jones, R. Sloman (captain), G. Hesketh, A. Johnson.

Northern Rugby League — Final Tie.

Featherstone Rovers
:: v. Swinton ::

AT WATERSHEDDINGS, OLDHAM
On Saturday May 5th, 1928.

:: PAVILION TEA TICKET. ::

Watersheddings hosted the 1928 Championship final, in which Swinton beat Featherstone Rovers 11-8 in front of a 15,451 crowd.

Above: This photograph is of the Second Test of the 1928 tour, held on the magnificent Sydney Cricket Ground. Oldham's giant forward Bob Sloman is under the posts wearing a skullcap. The Lions beat the Kangaroos 8-0 to clinch the Ashes.

Right: Tommy 'Guardsman' Rees, who had played 4 times for the Welsh RU international side before signing for Oldham, turned out to be one of the Roughyeds' most consistent players. This fine goal-kicking full-back played in 419 matches between 1928 and 1944, including an unbroken run of 121 games. The availability of Wigan's mercurial full-back Jim Sullivan limited Rees' Great Britain appearances to just one, playing against the Australian tourists of 1929/30. His 93 goals during 1933/34 was, at the time, a club record.

While he left Watersheddings in 1939 to sign for Broughton Rangers he continued to guest for Oldham throughout the Second World War.

Left: On 21 January 1933 a nineteen-year-old Welsh union scrum-half from the Cross Keys club pulled on a red and white Oldham shirt for the first time. The match, at home against Barrow, would be the beginning of an association between club and player that would span more than half a century. Alex Givvons, born in Newport, joined a large contingent of Welsh players at Watersheddings, one of the reasons that he chose the Roughyeds. He played in 241 Oldham first-team matches, interrupted only by a short spell spent with the Huddersfield club, was capped 6 times for Wales and also, in the attempt to establish the sport in France, toured twice with a RL XIII. Givvons served the Roughyeds both as player and coach and in January 1993, sixty years after joining the club, still served the Watersheddings side as a member of the back-room staff.

Right: The Roughyeds were usually awarded a match against any touring side that came to these shores but they played the 1933/34 Kangaroos twice, the 'green and golds' winning both by a comfortable margin. This photograph is of a collection of Australian tour shirts presented to the club down the years, including one from the 1933/34 tour.

Right: During the mid-1930s the Rugby League made efforts to establish the sport in France, which included English clubs playing promotional matches both here and on the Continent. Oldham, for instance, played Villeneuve at Watersheddings. The club also provided a number of players for exhibition tours, in particular from its Welsh contingent of Norman Pugh (pictured), Mick Downey, Alex Givvons and Lewis Rees, with Pugh, Rees and Givvons also playing regularly for the full Welsh international side that annually contested an England/France/Wales triangular tournament.

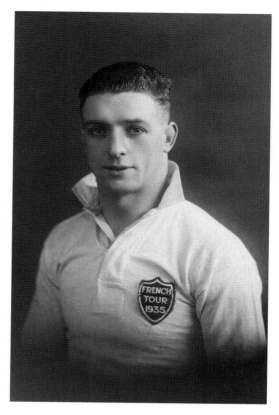

Below: Roughyeds in the snow! An Oldham side just prior to the outbreak of the Second World War. From left to right, back row: Garnett, Hall, Schofield, Ambler, Moore, Elson, Pugh, Brooks. Front row: Rhydderch, Mitchell, Read, Downey, Griffiths, Turner.

Right: Hooker Edgar Brooks signed for Oldham from the local Watersheddings junior side. He made his debut against the 1933/34 Australian tourists and would carry on playing for the club for the next seventeen years. He represented England on 3 occasions.

Below: Billy Stott was a goal-kicking centre born in Featherstone and signed in 1939 from Broughton Rangers. A classy footballer, whose career was interrupted by the Second World War, he played 81 first-team matches for Oldham before signing for Wakefield Trinity. He then became the inaugural winner of the Lance Todd Trophy when he starred for the Yorkshire side in the 1946 Challenge Cup final against Wigan. The photograph is of Stott in later years being presented with the match ball from that final.

five

The Second
World War

Above: Unlike during the First World War, when playing sport outside the armed services was looked upon as bordering on being unpatriotic, the Government encouraged organised sporting events as a diversion to the mundane. During the First World War Oldham closed down completely for one season but, during the whole of the Second World War, the club won the struggle to offer a reasonable quality of rugby league to the people of Oldham most weekends. Bolstered by guest players, amateurs and players from overseas forces stationed throughout the North-West, the club beat off the problems caused by conscription, essential war efforts and other obvious hardships.

The Rugby League endeavoured to play all its major competitions, although the Lancashire Cup was abandoned after 1940. Oldham, Barrow, St Helens, Wigan and Swinton were invited to play in the Yorkshire Cup!

Three of the club's young players were killed; Edward Bates, a half-back whose father had played for Oldham in the 1920s, Jack Hearne, a loose forward who had made his first-team debut in 1940 and Oldham-born Jack Mitchell.

The photograph is of prisoners of war working on a snowbound Watersheddings.

Left: Artful stand-off Willie Horne guested for the Roughyeds in two matches over the Christmas period of 1942. The sport's top young half-back was pursued by Oldham to sign on a permanent basis but instead chose his native Barrow, progressing to become one of the greatest halves of all time.

six

Following Hostilities

The period immediately after the Second World War was one of consolidation for the Oldham side, and it would be a further eight years before it reached a major final. However, this period was to produce a number of players who carved out a place for themselves in the history of the club while unknowingly helping place in position the springboard from which to launch the famous footballing side of the 1950s.

Welsh second-row forward Doug Phillips was selected for the 1946 tour, local-born prop Tommy Rostron played for both Lancashire and England, the club's centres Norman Harris and Ernie Large, along with young forward Harry Ogden, played for a British RL XIII and forward Les Thomas, signed from the Llanelli union side in 1946, played for both Wales and Great Britain. The photograph is of the Oldham side of 1946. Standing: Sutcliffe, Wood, Rostron, Ogden, Frost, Ayres, Shaw, Inglesfield, Heywood (trainer), G.F. Hutchins (official). Seated: Lees, Rees, Harris, Pugh (captain), Gummer, Griffiths, Kenny.

Opposite: The tall and powerful second-row forward Douglas Versailles Phillips made his debut for Oldham in 1945 and played only seven matches before being selected for the 1946 tour. The ex-Swansea union man played in each of the three Tests against the Australians, bringing home the Ashes. On his return the Welshman played only 11 matches for the club before being transferred to Belle Vue Rangers, from where he won a place on the 1950 tour.

Above: An action photograph of Doug Phillips, taken during the 1946 tour.

Left: The Gus Risman-led Lions forced an 8-8 draw in the First Test held in Sydney but went on to win the second, held in Brisbane, 14-5. Back on Sydney Cricket Ground the Ashes were secured when the British pulled off a magnificent 20-7 victory in the third and final Test. Phillips played in the second-row in each of the three encounters.

Above, left: Sixteen-year-old local forward Harry Ogden joined Oldham in 1940 and would amass 429 first-team appearances for the club over a sixteen-year period. This reliable prop-forward became the mainstay of the Roughyeds pack, playing in the 1954 Lancashire Cup and 1955 Championship finals. Alas, Ogden's only representative honour was to tour France with a British RL XIII in 1946.

Above, right: Norman Harris, a three-quarter signed from the Cross Keys union club in 1945, played 119 matches for the Roughyeds and 4 for Wales. He was selected for the 1946 tour trials but didn't make the cut. Transferred to Leigh in 1949, he later became coach to Rochdale Hornets. Norman's grandson is Great Britain international Iestyn Harris.

Right: Norman Harris' Welsh international cap, awarded after his appearance against France in Swansea in 1947. In front of a 20,000 crowd Wales won 17-15, with Harris scoring one of the three Welsh tries.

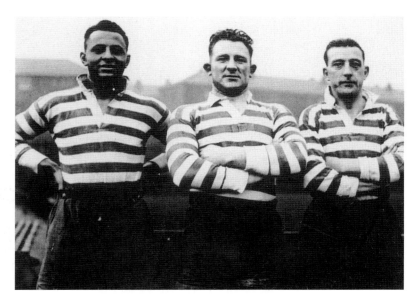

William John Moore, the Bridgend union and Welsh international lock, was a regular member of the Oldham front row both before and after the Second World War. This tough, no-nonsense forward played 158 first-team matches for the club and was also a boxer of some repute. He is photographed here standing between fellow Welshmen Alex Givvons and Mick Downey.

At the end of the 1948/49 season Oldham took part in a match against Salford, held in Lancaster, to help promote the sport in the area. The club's captain, Joe Mahoney, is seen here collecting the trophy. A three-quarter born in Cardiff, Mahoney signed in 1946 from the Northampton RU and was selected for the Welsh international side that played England at Wigan in 1948. After playing 67 matches for the club he joined Dewsbury in 1949.

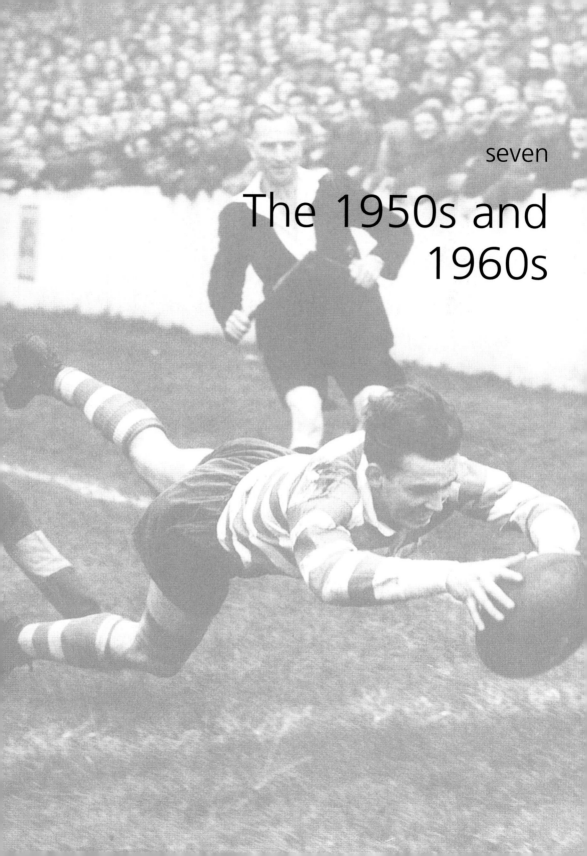

seven

The 1950s and 1960s

By the 1951/52 season Oldham had signed a combination of brilliant young players and experienced 'old heads' that would blend together into one of the most exciting football sides to have ever represented the club, winning the 1956/57 Championship as well as ending the season top of the Rugby League in both 1956/57 and 1957/58.

Three-quarter Alan Davies; scrum-half Frank Pitchford; goal-kicking full-back Bernard Ganley; the brilliant Welsh ball-handling forward Charlie Winslade; hooker Jack Keith; prop-forward Ken Jackson; winger Terry O'Grady; Cumbrian union forward Sid Little; fiery Welshman Bryn Day; a forward signed from Belle Vue Rangers; Warrington-born packman Arthur Tomlinson; utility player Frank Daley; brilliant half-back Frank Stirrup and yet another Welshman; ball-playing loose-forward and natural-born leader Bryn Goldswain, signed from Hull KR, would together mould into a team that would entertain rugby league supporters throughout the North.

In absolute contrast the club ended the 1969/70 season next to the bottom of a thirty-team division propped up by only Blackpool Borough. Oldham were forced to sell club captain Geoff Fletcher to Wigan and crowd favourite Derek Whitehead to Warrington to ease the financial burden. This was at a club that had dominated the local sporting scene for the last ninety years.

The photo is of an Oldham side from the 1951/52 season. From left to right, back row: F. Daley, A. Davies, B. Day, S. Little, H. Ogden, C. Winslade, J. Keith, W. Ganley. Front row: L. Platt, W. Mitchell, B. Goldswain (captain), J. Warham, F. Stirrup.

Above: Laurie Platt, the winger renowned for his diving tries. This local player, signed just after the Second World War, scored 64 tries from his 128 first-team outings and during the 1951/52 season twice represented Lancashire.

Right: It was said that Bryn Goldswain had flown eighty-three operational flights into Germany during the war and luckily for Oldham supporters, despite an offer from the RAF to make flying a career, he chose teaching. Bryn Goldswain was playing for Hull KR while studying to become a teacher in Liverpool and found the travelling to and from Humberside almost impossible, a factor in Oldham's favour when negotiating to bring him to Watersheddings. One of the most influential players that has ever represented the Roughyeds, Goldswain was instrumental in changing the early 1950s Oldham side into an entertaining and football-playing entity, the hallmark of any Oldham XIII that would take to the field during the next ten years. He played 228 matches for Oldham before retiring from playing in 1956. While at Watersheddings he represented Wales on 11 occasions and Other Nationalities once. He later coached at Blackpool, Rochdale Hornets and Doncaster.

Above: When half-back Frank Stirrup was brought in from the Salford club during season 1950/51 at the age of twenty-four he was certainly no old-head, but already a player who had the ability to link forwards and backs and knew every move in the book, some of which he had invented himself. He would take over as skipper from Goldswain and become the first Oldham player to hold aloft a major trophy for twenty years.

Right: Frank Stirrup and Clive Churchill lead out the Oldham and Australian sides at Watersheddings in 1952. Nineteen thousand spectators watched an exciting 7-7 draw, one of only two games from a 22-match programme against club sides that the tourists failed to win.

Opposite: Alan Davies, signed from Leigh amateur side Dootsons, made his Watersheddings debut in 1950 against Wakefield Trinity. Perhaps the finest centre ever to play for Oldham, Davies would also become the club's most-capped player, representing Great Britain on 20 occasions, England on 2 and Lancashire 17. He played in four Lancashire Cup and two Championship finals for the Roughyeds, toured in 1958 and was a member of both the 1957 and 1960 World Cup squads, helping lift the trophy in the second of those two series. He played 391 first-team matches for the Roughyeds before being transferred to Wigan in 1961.

Above: Oldham reached the 1954 Lancashire Cup final, in which they faced Barrow. Played on Swinton's Station Road ground in front of a 25,000 crowd, the Roughyeds suffered an unexpected 12-2 reversal. *Below:* Their luck was still out when, during the same season, they took on Warrington in the Championship final in Manchester. On a mudflat of a Maine Road pitch, watched by 49,000 spectators the Wire, who had won 5 and drawn 1 of the last 6 meetings between the two clubs, won a closely fought encounter 7-3. It was forty-four years since the Watersheddings side had lifted the Championship but it wouldn't be too long before the disappointed Oldham fans would see this put to rights.

Opposite: One of the most accurate goal-kickers the sport has known, the ex-Leigh Spinners full-back Bernard Ganley was the first Oldham player to break through the 100-goals-in-a-season barrier when, during 1951/52 (his first full season with the club), he kicked 106. He was the first in the game to pass the 200-in-a-season mark when during season 1957/58 he kicked 219, a record that he would hold until Salford's David Watkins kicked 221 during season 1972/73. His 14 goals against Liverpool in 1959 still stands as an Oldham club record and the 10 that he kicked for Great Britain against France in 1957 equalled the Great Britain record then held by Leeds' Lewis Jones. Ganley played 341 first-team matches for Oldham, kicked a total of 1,358 goals and scored 15 tries. He also played 3 times for both Great Britain and Lancashire before retiring from playing in 1961.

THE NORTHERN RUGBY FOOTBALL LEAGUE

League Championship Final

WARRINGTON v. OLDHAM

SATURDAY MAY 14th
Kick-off 3 p.m.

At Maine Road
Manchester

OFFICIAL PROGRAMME - - - Price 6d.

Above: Oldham centre Alan Davies attempts to ward off Warrington's winger Brian Bevan during the 1955 Championship final, but is hampered by the Manchester mud.

Left: Terry O'Grady, who signed for the Roughyeds from local amateur side St Mary's, had a sensational start to his professional rugby career, the seventeen-year-old being selected for the Lancashire County side to play the 1951 touring New Zealanders. Three years later he was chosen for the 1954 tour to Australia and New Zealand, scoring 28 tries and playing in five out of the six Tests. The following season the three-quarter partnership of Davies and O'Grady scored 51 tries for the Roughyeds but from there on the winger was troubled by injuries and was eventually transferred to Wigan.

Prop-forward Ken Jackson signed for Oldham in 1950 from the local amateur side Waterhead and the following season won Lancashire honours. It would, however, be 1953/54 before the robust forward could count on being an automatic choice. The open-side prop and hooker partnership of Jackson and Keith would usually provide the Oldham backs with far more than their fair share of the ball, often the difference between victory and defeat. Jackson was chosen for the 1958 tour but while in Australia unfortunately picked up an injury, forcing his premature departure home. He played twice for Great Britain, once for Lancashire and, between 1950 and 1961, 243 matches for Oldham.

One of the most popular players that has ever represented the club, big second-row forward Charlie Winslade superseded Bryn Goldswain as the ball-player of the Oldham pack. Signed in 1950 from the Maesteg union club, the Welshman immediately made an impact and would be almost ever-present throughout the decade. Winslade played in all of Oldham's big games of that era, was selected to play twice for a British representative XIII, 4 times for Wales and once for Great Britain as well as a massive 358 matches for the Roughyeds before joining Warrington in 1961. After his death, Winslade's ashes were scattered on the Watersheddings pitch and in later years one of the streets within the new housing development that was built on the site of the old ground was named in his memory.

Above: Lanky young hooker Jack Keith, signed out of Leeds junior rugby in 1949, was one of the characters in the sport during the 1950s. Never short of confidence, Keith was one of the best hookers of a ball in the game and rarely failed to monopolise the scrums. In the loose he was just as effective, an elusive runner (who often entertained the Watersheddings crowd by giving the impression that he didn't quite know his own intentions!) and impressive ball-handler, scoring 63 tries from his 342 first-team outings. The hooker, sporting an eye wound, is pictured here receiving the Lancashire Cup from Oldham's mayor, Councillor Arnold Tweedale.

Left: Hooker Jack Keith scores against Rochdale Hornets.

Opposite, below: Try-scoring scrum-half Frank Pitchford is helped to his feet by winger John Etty. Oldham's forward trio of Winslade, Jackson and Keith look on. In the background is winger Dick Cracknell.

Above: The three Oldham stalwarts Ken Jackson, Charlie Winslade and Jack Keith share a well-earned benefit. They are seen here receiving their cheques from the mayor of Oldham, Alderman G.F. Holden. Oldham coach Gus Risman is stood next to Jack Keith.

During the 1956/57 season Oldham topped both the Rugby League and Lancashire League, won the Championship, lifted the Lancashire Cup and won the A.J. Law Cup, a trophy played for annually against neighbours Rochdale Hornets. From left to right, back row: Heywood (trainer), Mitchell (trainer), Vines, Winslade, Keith, Shaw (staff), Little, Turner, Jackson, Jarman, Edwards, Navesey (physio), Jenkins (coach). Front row: Cracknell, Davies, Daley, Ganley, Stirrup (captain), Pitchford, Ayres, Etty.

Club captain Frank Stirrup collects the 1956 Lancashire Cup after his side beat St Helens 10-3 in the final held at Central Park, Wigan. St Helens' coach Jim Sullivan said, 'I think Oldham just about had the edge on us today. Both clubs are ten points better than any other teams in the league.'

A massive crowd of 62,217 watched Oldham win the 1956/57 Championship by beating Hull 15-14 at Odsal Stadium, Bradford. Hull's winger Stan Cowan scored a try in the dying minutes, only to watch his full-back Colin Hutton fail with a relatively easy conversion kick that, if he had succeeded, would have meant the cup going to The Boulevard. The action shot is of three-quarter Dennis Ayres scoring one of Oldham's three tries.

From left to right: John Etty, Frank Stirrup (Championship), Bernard Ganley (Lancashire League), Alan Davies (Lancashire Cup) and Charlie Winslade (A.J. Law) parade the four-cup haul of 1956/57.

THE NORTHERN RUGBY FOOTBALL LEAGUE

LEAGUE CHAMPIONSHIP FINAL

HULL v. OLDHAM

SATURDAY
8th MAY
1957

Kick-off 3.00 p.m.

At ODSAL STADIUM
BRADFORD

OFFICIAL SOUVENIR PROGRAMME - Price 6d.

The Championship victory of 1956/57 was the first time that Oldham had won the trophy for forty-six years, and it would be the last.

Season 1957/58 saw Oldham finish top of the Rugby League for the second consecutive season, winning 31 and drawing one of their 38-match programme, as well as holding on to both the Lancashire League Championship and the Lancashire Cup. The photograph is of Wigan's out-half Billy Boston showing a clean pair of heels to the Oldham defence in the final. Mind you, this was a rare break for the winger-cum-half-back, who was given such a torrid time by the Roughyeds' out-half Frank Daley that he was eventually forced out onto the wing. The match, won 13-8 by Oldham, was played in front of almost 43,000 spectators at Swinton.

During the 1957/58 season Great Britain played France on three occasions, winning them all. Oldham's Bernard Ganley, Alan Davies, Ken Jackson, Sid Little and Derek Turner played in the first game, held in Toulouse, and kept their places for the second at Wigan, a match in which Bernard Ganley kicked 10 goals, a then-record haul against the French. The photograph is of the team that played at Wigan and is, from left to right, standing: Dennis Goodwin, Phil Jackson, Derek Turner, Ken Jackson, Mick Sullivan, Tommy Harris, Bernard Ganley. Front: Alan Davies, Alan Prescott, Sid Little, Jeff Stevenson, Dave Bolton, Billy Boston.

Oldham completed a hat-trick of wins when the side held on to the Lancashire Cup for the third consecutive season, beating St Helens 12-2 in the 1958/59 final at Swinton. Oldham's loose-forward Derek Turner is seen here attempting to charge down an Alex Murphy kick.

In March 1959 Oldham paid Workington a world-record transfer fee of £10,650 to secure the services of international winger Ike Southward. He found life away from his native Cumbria difficult but from his 52 first-team matches the dynamic wingman scored 54 tries. A veteran of the 1958 tour, Southward continued his international and county career during his short spell at Watersheddings, playing 6 matches for Great Britain and 2 for Cumberland. The homesick Southward was transferred back to Workington in 1960, breaking the world-record transfer for a second time, the £11,002 10s fee topping the £11,000 that St Helens had recently paid Wigan for winger Mick Sullivan. The photograph is of Southward supported by centre Brian Lord in a match against Featherstone in 1960.

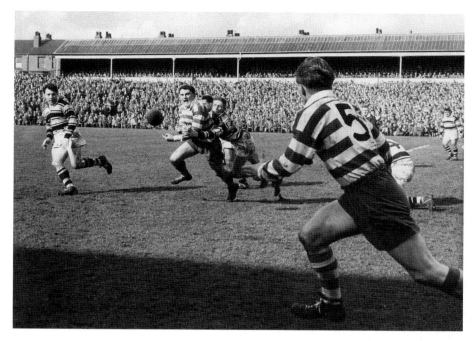

Following the world-record-fee signing of winger Ike Southward, Oldham quickly returned to Cumberland, this time to Whitehaven, paying out a then-record fee for a forward when they negotiated a £9,000 deal for back-rower Geoff Robinson, outstripping the previous record of £8,000 that Wakefield had recently paid Oldham for the signature of loose-forward Derek Turner. The tall and fast Robinson settled in town far easier than Southward, playing 177 matches for the first team between 1959 and 1965 before signing for Warrington.

The 1960 World Cup was contested in Great Britain between Australia, France, Great Britain and New Zealand. Oldham's centre Alan Davies played in each of the Lions' three matches, topping the league table with 6 points to take the trophy. Davies is photographed, supported by Frank Myler, scoring a try against France at Swinton.

Dave Parker, the excellent ball-handling Lancashire union captain, signed for Oldham from Manchester in 1960. He was a clever footballer who could seek out the gap and then had the speed to go through it and was also renowned for his perfectly timed low tackles. Parker, a natural leader, was soon promoted to club captain. Although during his seven seasons at the club the side never won a trophy, this excellent ambassador for the Roughyeds gained both county and international honours. The photograph was taken in a match against Australia at Watersheddings in 1963.

A landmark of the old Watersheddings ground was the scoreboard. Added in the second half of the 1950s it was state of the art and the envy of most clubs. Hard to believe now!

Peter Smethurst had three spells at Watersheddings, the first as a player and the second and third as coach. In either role he never gave less than 100 per cent. The £4,000 that Oldham paid Swinton for his signature in 1961 must rank as one of the shrewdest transfer deals the club has ever negotiated. A utility player, equally at home in the centre as in the second-row, Smethurst's trademark was to come out of the tackle with a grin on his face, a trait that hardly ever failed to irritate the opposing defence. He was one of the club's finest ever captains, perhaps best illustrated during the 1966 Lancashire Cup final, when Wigan were expected to win by a cricket score. Instead, with just seconds remaining, Oldham back Stan McLeod was inches short of touching down for a match-winning try, the Central Park outfit being relieved to hang on to a 16-13 scoreline. Smethurst had led his troops like a latter-day Wellington.

This photograph is of the squad that featured in the 1964 Challenge Cup semi-final and its two replays against Hull KR. From left to right, standing: Harry Major, Stuart Whitehead, Brian Lord, Charlie Bott, Johnny Noon, Geoff Robinson, Ken Wilson, Dave Parker, Len McIntyre. Sitting: John Donovan, Geoff Sims, Frank Dyson, Peter Smethurst, Trevor Simms. Kneeling: Jack Pycroft, Vince Nestor. The first match at Headingley ended 5-5, the first replay at Swinton finished prematurely 17-14 in Oldham's favour (it was abandoned by referee Dennis Davies during the second stanza of extra time due to the failing light) and finally Hull KR ran out 12-2 winners in the second and final replay at Huddersfield.

The Oldham trophy cabinet remained empty throughout the 1960s, despite the club appearing in the 1960 and 1964 Challenge Cup semi-finals and both the 1966 and 1968 Lancashire Cup finals. Despite the shortage of silverware, the period will be best remembered for the introduction of a number of players who would form the backbone of the side for years to come. Winger Mike Elliott (446 matches), centre Phil Larder (328 matches), prop-forward Ken Wilson (321 matches), hooker Kevin Taylor (429 matches), full-back Martin Murphy (462 matches) and second-row forward Bob Irving (296 matches) all came into the team at this time.

Right: Front-row forward Ken 'Tug' Wilson, born in Newark, had represented the RAF, Combined Services, Gloucestershire and England at union before signing for Oldham in 1963. If a hand injury had not put paid to a promising career as a heavyweight boxer the Roughyeds would have missed out completely on this workaholic forager who would serve the club through ten seasons, his ball-winning front-row partnership with hooker Kevin Taylor being legendary.

Above: Signed as a sixteen-year-old from the local Werneth Continuation side, hooker Kevin Taylor made his first-team debut just prior to his seventeenth birthday in 1963. His 429 first-team appearances for the club have been bettered by no more than five other players and his try-scoring ability, coupled to his magnificent support game, ensured he was regularly among the club's leading try-scorers. He gave over twelve years' service to the Watersheddings side, along the way gaining Lancashire and England honours before signing for Leigh in 1977.

Wilf Briggs, the Oldham stand-off signed from the Leigh club, who could turn a game on its head. One of the best try-poachers of the 1960s, Briggs touched down 44 times in 73 first-team matches, a tries to appearance record only surpassed by Oldham's great wingmen.

Opposite, above: Mike Elliott's 446 appearances for the club is a record for a three-quarter. Signed at the age of seventeen from the Cwmcllyn union side, the Welshman made his debut against Wakefield Trinity in 1962. This was the beginning of a seventeen-year association, the winger topping the club's leading try-scorer chart on six occasions, scoring a total of 153 tries. The photograph is of Mike Elliot and Kevin Taylor being presented with well-earned benefit cheques from club chairman Arthur Walker.

Left: Phil Larder.

PHIL LARDER

OLDHAM   R L F C
1968–1979

TESTIMONIAL BROCHURE

Above: Oldham-born three-quarter Phil Larder didn't turn to rugby until his late teens, having attended a soccer-playing school. Graduating through the same Werneth Continuation rugby league side as Kevin Taylor, Larder then focused his attention on the other code, spending some time with Oldham RU club before being enticed to join grade-one side Broughton Park. Via Loughborough College, Sale and Lancashire, the classy back signed for Oldham in 1968. Besides being a prolific try-scorer Larder was also an accomplished goal-kicker, the combination making him one of the club's most prolific point-scoring three-quarters in its history. His partnership with winger Mike Elliott spanned eleven seasons, proving to be one of the club's most productive playing partnerships. Phil Larder joined Whitehaven, where he ended his playing career at the age of thirty-seven. He has since made a name for himself as a first-class rugby coach, spending time at Keighley, Sheffield Eagles and Widnes, and was also Director of Coaching with the Rugby League before once again turning his eye to union, where he progressed to become assistant coach to the England side.

This painting by Steve Bennett is of Oldham's full-back Martin Murphy, who made his debut against his hometown club Leigh in 1966. This pocket-dynamo player, who had the ability to both time tackles to perfection and shoot through the slightest of gaps, soon became a favourite with the Watersheddings crowd, which he would continue to entertain for sixteen years. Capped by Lancashire, he also made one appearance for England when he scored a last-minute try to secure an 11-9 victory against the French in Perpignan in 1975. 'Murph's' 462 appearances for the Roughyeds is a post-war record.

Bob Irving was just sixteen years old when, in 1965, he put pen to paper to sign for Oldham, having previously played union for the Huddersfield club and league for St Joseph's amateur side. This second-row forward, who had a combination of strength and speed, made his first-team debut the same year that he signed, making him one of the youngest players ever to represent the club. The blockbusting Yorkshireman was soon in the honours, quickly progressing through the county side and Great Britain Under-24s and, by the end of 1967, had played twice for Great Britain against France and in three Tests against the touring Australians. In 1970 he toured Australia and New Zealand and was a member of the 1972 World Cup squad that lifted the trophy in France. By the time he joined Wigan in 1972 he had played 11 matches for Great Britain and 3 for England. Later in his career he played for Salford, Blackpool (as coach) and Barrow. Sadly, Bob died in 1999 aged 51.

1966, and the Oldham club breaks new ground, announcing the opening of its new social club and money-spinning nightspot.

OLDHAM RUGBY
SOCIAL CLUB

WATERSHEDDINGS

Leads the League with Top Stars in
Variety, Pop and Disco.

THURSDAY:
DISCO—Graham Don Donna

FRIDAY and SATURDAY:
EARLY EXPRESSION
TOMMY LANE
RAY LEWIS
JOHN HARVEY

THURSDAY, November 2
DISCO—Graham Don Donna
FRIDAY and SATURDAY,
November 3 and 4:
CAPRICORN
KARNHAM OF INDIA
GERRY BENTON

And don't forget to book your table for a meal at our wonderful restaurant — Our chef specialises in Wedding feasts.

Above, left: A paltry 3,329 Saturday afternoon crowd turned out at Watersheddings to watch the touring Australians beat the Roughyeds 18-8, reflecting a general decline in attendances throughout the league.

Above, right: Sunday rugby was high on the agenda in most rugby league boardrooms as attendances were dropping at an alarming rate. Oldham's were no exception and the first Sunday game was scheduled for 24 March 1968 against Leigh, but had to be postponed due to a frozen pitch. It was the following December when Whitehaven were the visitors before the Roughyeds actually opened the turnstiles for Sunday rugby. The attendance of 2,021 was only slightly above the Saturday average.

Left: Despite the extra cash generated from the social side of the business, gates at Watersheddings were at an all-time low, and the club was forced to sell club captain and pack leader Geoff Fletcher to Wigan and utility back and vice-captain Derek Whitehead to Warrington. Only 6 of the 34 league matches were won and Oldham finished season 1969/70 next to the bottom of a league of thirty clubs, an unbelievable situation for a club of Oldham's pedigree. At the end of the season the committee and its chairman were voted out of office en bloc.

1969-70		P	W	D	L	F	A	Pts
1	Leeds	34	30	0	4	674	314	60
2	Castleford	34	25	1	8	493	298	51
3	St. Helens	34	23	1	10	702	292	47
4	Wigan	34	23	0	11	698	420	46
5	Hull K.R.	34	22	2	10	566	395	46
6	Salford	34	22	1	11	572	332	45
7	Leigh	34	21	3	10	554	325	45
8	Featherstone R.	34	22	1	11	558	385	45
9	Swinton	34	20	4	10	550	351	44
10	Widnes	34	21	2	11	473	355	44
11	Hull	34	20	2	12	420	357	42
12	Bradford N.	34	19	0	15	511	404	38
13	Whitehaven	34	18	2	14	404	450	38
14	Warrington	34	17	2	15	559	421	36
15	Huddersfield	34	17	1	16	377	395	35
16	Halifax	34	16	0	18	395	454	32
17	Batley	34	15	1	18	388	485	31
18	Bramley	34	14	1	19	374	498	29
19	Barrow	34	14	1	19	379	511	29
20	Rochdale H.	34	13	3	18	334	524	29
21	Wakefield T.	34	13	2	19	521	452	28
22	Dewsbury	34	13	1	20	383	451	27
23	Hunslet	34	13	1	20	391	574	27
24	Workington T.	34	12	2	20	416	483	26
25	Keighley	34	13	0	21	370	555	26
26	York	34	11	1	22	378	502	23
27	Doncaster	34	7	0	27	264	564	14
28	Huyton	34	5	3	26	177	643	13
29	Oldham	34	6	0	28	343	590	12
30	Blackpool B.	34	6	0	28	318	762	12

eight

The 1970s

Oldham went through the 1970s failing to reach the final of any of the major competitions. A two-division format was introduced for the 1973/74 season and Oldham were in the Second Division for four out of the six seasons that the system operated. The photograph is of the 1970/71 Oldham squad. From left to right, back row: Fletcher, Clark, Walker, Irving, Reynolds, Daley, Wilson, Sayer. Middle row: Taylor, Murphy, Starkey (captain), Larder, Garrett. Front row: Smith, mascot, Davies.

The only five-figure crowd at Watersheddings during the 1970s turned up to watch a Challenge Cup third round match against Widnes. An attendance of 11,503 saw the Chemics beat the Roughyeds in 1975. Here, half-back David Treasure takes on the Widnes defence.

While the 1970s was a decade of underachievement for the Roughyeds it did have its bright spots. Most supporters who can remember the period will recall 1972/73 as the Foster-Hill-Starkey season. Foster (pictured) and Hill controlled events on the field and coach Graham Starkey dealt with matters off it. Journeyman forward Foster, with his man-of-steel and firebrand reputation, had been signed from Barrow for £2,750 and silky ball-handling utility back Cliff Hill arrived from Wigan. Oldham won 20 and drew 2 of their 34-match programme to slot into ninth spot in a single division of thirty. Oldham would have finished higher if Hill had not suffered from injuries; 8 of their 12 defeats had been without Hill in the side. That season the team also reached the semi-final of the BBC2 Floodlit Trophy before losing 10-8 at Leigh.

The selection of the 1972 Great Britain World Cup squad, coached by Jim Challinor, who would soon join Oldham in a similar capacity, included Oldham's second-row forward Bob Irving. The Lions beat Australia 27-21 in Perpignan, the French 13-4 in Grenoble and New Zealand 53-19 in Pau to head the qualifying table. The final against Australia, staged in Lyon in front of a paltry crowd of 4,231, was level at 10-10 after eighty minutes, and despite extra time the score remained the same. The Lions were declared winners due to their higher position in the qualifying league table. Irving was used as a substitute for the final, replacing Leeds' David Jeanes. The shield, pictured here, was presented to Irving by the RL.

Ex-Featherstone Rovers, Bradford Northern, Hull KR, Leeds and Great Britain ball-playing Test prop Terry Clawson was signed from the Headingley club for £3,750 in time for the opening of the 1973/74 season, during which he was selected for each of the three Tests against the touring Australians. Clawson was sufficiently successful against the Kangaroos to force his selection for the 1974 tour, where he played in two of the Tests against Australia and in two of the Tests against New Zealand. On his return Clawson demanded a transfer and, after playing a total of just 22 first-team matches for Oldham, the journeyman forward signed for York.

TUG WILSON
SOUVENIR PROGRAMME

1963

1975

OLDHAM
v
ENGLAND

April 22nd 1975 Kick off 7-30

Programme   10p

Left: The England side, preparing for the 1975 World Championship, beat Oldham 27-5 at Watersheddings in a benefit match held for stalwart prop Ken Wilson.

Below: Oldham's half-back David Treasure was selected to represent Wales during the 1975 World Championship, playing in four of Wales' games and being a non-playing substitute in a fifth. Australia won the tournament.

Centenary
Season

OLDHAM
v
LEEDS

SUNDAY 12th SEPTEMBER
Kick Off 3-30 p.m.

TODAY'S MATCH BALL
presented by
SADDLEWORTH SPORTS CENTRE
Chew Valley Road
Greenfield

10p

It was 100 years since Abraham Fletcher and Co. had roped off Sugar Meadow
for Oldham's first ever match, turning out in their bumblebee strip against near-
neighbours Stalybridge. There had since been both the good times and the bad,
but this, the Centenary Season, would be one of the toughest of them all. There
were pressing financial difficulties, the side suffered early exits from each of the cup
competitions and by winning just 7 of their 30 league matches were firmly rooted
at the bottom of the First Division and relegated. The worst was yet to come
when coach Jim Challinor, who had suffered illness throughout the season, never
recovered from his ailments and sadly died.

nine

The 1980s

Oldham supporters were pleased to ring out the 1970s but, ironically, the club had just hit on a new and exciting lottery that, by the turn of the decade, was beginning to bring in much-needed revenue. Wisely, a good proportion of this funding was invested in youth. The team photograph is of the 1980 Colts, which includes Ray Ashton, Andy Goodway, Mick Worrall and Terry Flanagan, all of whom went on to gain selection for the 1984 tour, and Paddy Kirwan, who played for Lancashire.

Season 1985/86 saw the Roughyeds end their campaign fifth in the First Division, their highest league position since the 1950s. Twice during the decade the side reached both the semi-finals of the Challenge Cup and the John Player Trophy. They reached the final of the Lancashire Cup in 1986 and 1989 and won a Divisional Final at Old Trafford but, while the club had entered the new decade on the back of an enterprising and exciting money-spinning lottery, it would depart it with the disappointment that the £750,000 share issue that would have hopefully transferred the club into a thriving PLC was only a little over a third taken up, compounding the ever-pressing financial burden.

From left to right, standing: Brian Gartland (coach), M. Edwards, J. Johnson, T. Wood, P. Vincent, A. Goodway, J. Walls, M. Coombes, P. D'Adamo, M. Worrall, T. Flanagan, Derek Foy (coach). Kneeling: S. Littler, J. Warburton, P. Kirwan, S. Dobb, R. Ashton.

The signing of Rosslyn Park's England union international forward Bob Mordell and Harlequins' captain Adrian Alexander at the end of 1979 took most Oldham supporters by surprise but caused more than just a stir in southern union circles. Without warning, an unfashionable rugby league club had scooped up two of their most formidable forwards.

The Oldham side that opened the 1980s. From left to right, standing: Ray Ashton, Brian Lockwood, Ray Martland, Geoff Clarkson, Adrian Alexander, Bob Mordell, Mick Parrish, Terry Flanagan, Steve Herbert. Kneeling: Martin Murphy, Geoff Munro, Bill Francis, Clive Hunter, Ken Gwilliam, Clive Sullivan. Mascot: Adrian Blackburn.

Left: Mick Parrish, a powerful twenty-two-year-old centre, had played for Hunslet and Yorkshire before he signed for Oldham for an £18,500 fee. While with Hunslet, the highly rated goal-kicker had the distinction of scoring in every one of the Yorkshire club's matches played during the 1979/80 season, and repeated the feat during season 1981/82, this time with the Roughyeds, when he scored 17 tries and kicked 164 goals. He kicked a total of 566 goals and scored 37 tries from his 191 Oldham appearances.

Above: Under new coach Frank Myler, Oldham won the 1981/82 Second Division Championship. The photograph is of winger Geoff Munro, who played in 21 consecutive matches during the season.

The 1982/83 season was the most successful at Watersheddings since 1960/61, Oldham finishing eighth in a sixteen-team First Division, losing narrowly to leaders Hull at The Boulevard in the play-offs. Terry Flanagan and Andy Goodway were selected for Great Britain for a two-match tournament against France, Ray Ashton and Mick Worrall for the Great Britain Under-24 side and Stephen Dobbs, Paul Lowndes and Alan Platt were selected for the Colts tour to Papua New Guinea and Australia. The photograph is of Oldham forward Andy Goodway in action.

Oldham had a club-record five players selected for the 1984 tour to Australia and New Zealand. Second-row forwards Andy Goodway and Mick Worrall, centre Des Foy and scrum-half Ray Ashton (pictured left) were among the original selections, with loose-forward Terry Flanagan added when St Helens' forward Chris Arkwright pulled out due to injury.

Great Britain coach Frank Myler shocked the rugby league world when he selected Oldham centre Des Foy at stand-off and Ellery Hanley out on the wing for the First Test against the Kangaroos, held on Sydney Cricket Ground in 1984. Oldham forwards Worrall and Goodway were also selected for the match, won 25-8 by the Australians. The Oldham second-row pair kept their places for the Second Test in Brisbane, which the home side won 18-6 to take the Ashes, but only Andy Goodway kept his place for the Third Test back on Sydney Cricket Ground, failing to stop the Australians completing a clean sweep. The photograph below is of Terry Flanagan, who played in the Third Test against New Zealand and also against Papua New Guinea.

Dedicated, enthusiastic and bloody-minded with the heart of a lion, scheming scrum half Paddy Kirwan was just a half-yard of pace away from being the Great Britain scrum half of the 1980s. While being selected at the base of the scrum for Great Britain Colts, Kirwan was also dipping his toe into first-team rugby. A friendly rivalry developed between the local-born scrum half and Ray Ashton, the pair eventually ousting the established Bill Francis and Ken Gwilliam. Paddy, who was awarded a Lancashire cap, was not the luckiest of players where injuries were concerned, perhaps the worst moment of his rugby career being when he broke his leg in a match against Fulham in 1987. Kirwan will have his own favourite rugby moments but that now-famous try that he scored under the Watersheddings posts in the last minute of the game to knock the mighty Wigan side out of the 1987 Challenge Cup will live long in the memory of Oldham fans. He later became second-team coach during the club's Super League era and eventually first-team coach when the 'new' Oldham club was formed in 1997.

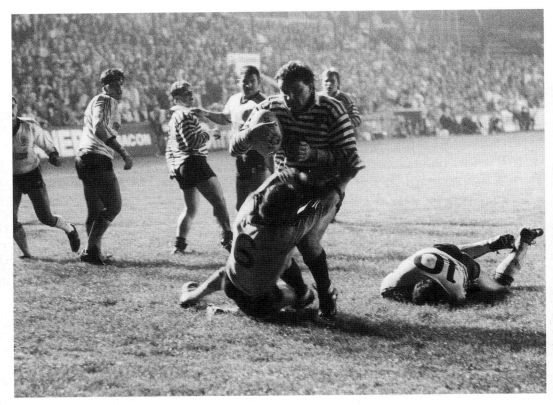

Great Britain's second-row forward David Hobbs had been awarded the Lance Todd Trophy while playing for Featherstone in the 1983 Challenge Cup final and had just returned from the 1984 tour when Oldham coach Frank Myler parted with £40,000 for his signature. This goal-kicking forward was seen as the ideal replacement for Andy Goodway, who had just left Watersheddings and signed for Wigan. Hobbs, who played twice for Great Britain while with the Roughyeds, helped Oldham to fifth spot in the First Division during the 1984/85 season, their highest position in the league since the halcyon days of the 1950s. Two seasons later, despite amassing 26 points, the Watersheddings side, which had that season competed in the Lancashire Cup final, were relegated despite ending the season in thirteenth position out of a first devision of 16. It was an absolutely stupid system that allowed a quarter of the sport's premier clubs to be relegated, Oldham ending the campaign just two points below Widnes in eighth spot. The photograph captures Hobbs during a typical Watersheddings night match.

Under a new coaching duo of Eric Fitzsimons and Iain McCorquodale, Oldham topped the 1987/88 Second Division table and beat Featherstone 28-26 in a wonderful topsy-turvy divisional final at Old Trafford. This changing room scene depicts, from left to right, back: Mike Ford, Des Foy, Ian Sherratt, Charlie McAlister, Leo Casey, Paul Lord. Front: Richard Irving, Gary Warnecke, Hugh Waddell, Keith Atkinson, Kevin Meadows, Mal Graham, Terry Flanagan, Colin Hawkyard, Paddy Kirwan. This photo was taken after beating Wakefield Trinity to secure promotion back to the First Division.

Oldham had two players, prop Hugh Waddell and scrum-half Mike Ford, selected for the 1988 tour to Papua New Guinea, Australia and New Zealand. Waddell played in the Lions' 26-12 win against the Kangaroos in the Third Test on Sydney Cricket Ground, the first win against Australia in sixteen matches, and also in the single Test Match against New Zealand in Christchurch. Mike Ford didn't make the Tests but played in 7 of the regional matches, scoring 5 tries. The photograph is of Hugh Waddell.

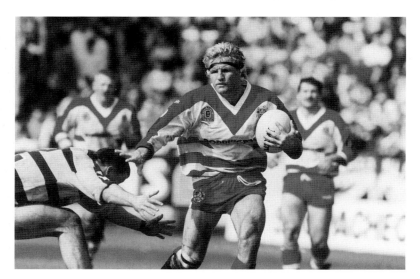

Season 1989/90 was one of the most exciting in the recent history of the club. The Tony Barrow-led squad reached the final of the Lancashire Cup, beating St Helens 36-6 in the quarter-final at Knowsley Road and then disposing of Wigan in a wonderful Watersheddings semi-final night match. In the Challenge Cup they beat World Club Champions Widnes 16-4 in front of their own fans on the way to the semi-finals. Then, to round off the season, came that magnificent divisional final at Old Trafford against league winners Hull KR. In a wonderful display of catch-up rugby the Watersheddings side beat the Robins 30-29 when Tommy Martyn scored Oldham's final try to reverse what had started out as a 29-6 deficit. The photograph is of Oldham's Australian loose forward John Cogger.

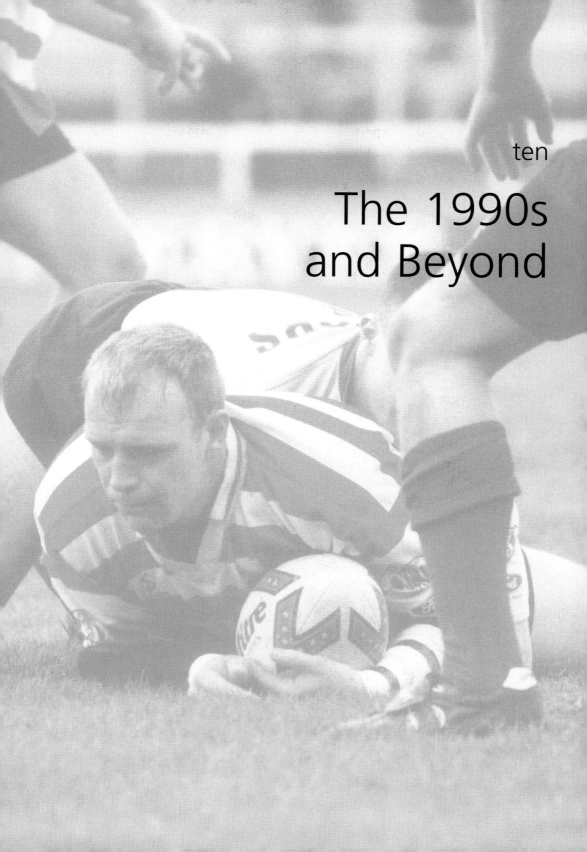

ten

The 1990s and Beyond

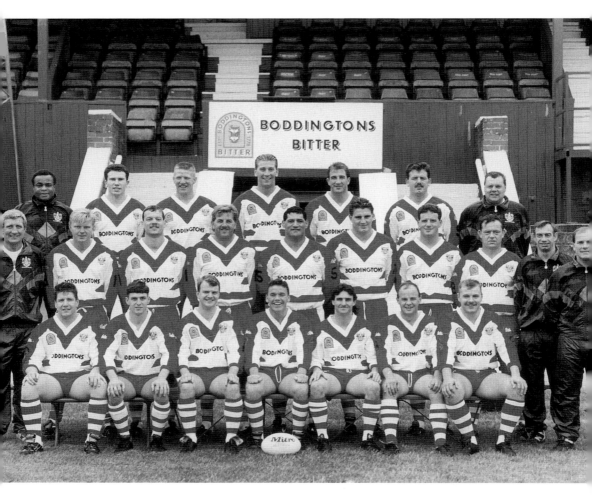

The Tony Barrow-led side that breezed into the 1990s failed to halt the club's steep financial slide. The greyhound track and the training pitch, both part of the Watersheddings complex, were sold off to relieve the burden, so the first whispers of Super League negotiations, and the heady levels of cash sponsorship from News Corporation that went with it, was akin to the expectancy of a decade of Christmas's to the Oldham board.

Andy Goodway led the side to tenth spot in the 1993/94 season's Stones Bitter Championship, which was good enough to force the RL to eventually award the club a place in the first-ever European Super League that would kick-off in early spring 1996. Between then and Christmas 1997 the Roughyeds had become the Bears; Watersheddings had been sold off and demolished; the side had played in the World Club Championships both here and in Australia; had finished bottom of Super League Two, been placed into voluntary liquidation resulting in a new club Oldham (1997) Ltd being formed and allocated a place in Division Two for the 1998 season.

The photograph is of the Oldham squad that opened the 1990/91 season. From left to right, back: Ossie Rowe (conditioner), Des Foy, John Fieldhouse, Tony Barrow jnr, John Henderson, Andy Ruane, John Watkins (physio). Middle: Tony Barrow (coach), Ronnie Duane, Gary Hyde, Paul Round, Charlie McAlister, Austin Donegan, Duncan Platt, Derek Pyke, Derek Whitehead (assistant coach), Ian Taylor (second-team coach). Front: Richard Russell, Paul Lord, Steve Robinson, Mike Ford (captain), Bret Clark, Paddy Kirwan, Trevor Croston.

Tourist scrum half Mike Ford leads the Roughyeds into the 1990s.

Above: A painting of Oldham winger Scott Ranson scoring one of the Roughyeds' four tries in the divisional final of 1992 at Old Trafford, which they lost 34-20 to Sheffield Eagles.

Left: Bobby Lindner, the forward who toured with both the 1986 and 1990 Kangaroos, signed to play for the Roughyeds for the 1993/94 season. Before the end of the campaign he had replaced fellow Australian Peter Tunks as Oldham's sixteenth coach in eighteen seasons. The dynamic Queenslander returned to Australia at the end of that campaign to be replaced as coach by Andy Goodway.

Right: During 1994/95 Andy Goodway and his assistant Alan McCurrie guided Oldham to tenth place in the Stones Bitter Championship, sufficient to unlock the door to European Super League and the cash that went along with it. It would kick-off in the spring of 1996 but, in order to celebrate the sport's centenary, there would first be a short winter season to be known as the Stones Bitter Centenary Championship. Encompassing the razzle-dazzle that went along with this new era Oldham unleashed the Bears in time for the home clash against Wigan, which the Bears won 28-26.

Above: Eight of the Bears' eleven home matches during the first summer-scheduled Super League season were played at Watersheddings and three at Boundary Park, producing an average attendance of 3,629, compared to a 3,889 average gate generated during the last full winter season. The Bears won 9 and drew one of their 22 fixtures to finish eighth. The photograph is of Bears' out-half Francis Maloney in action.

Text on plaque:

Watersheddings Rugby Groun[d]
On the site of the housing developme[nt]
to the east of this park was the famou[s]
Watersheddings rugby ground, which
served the Oldham club from its openi[ng]
on the 28th September 1889, until
the last first team match on
the 19th January 1997.

Above: This blue commemorative plaque unveiled by Oldham club chairman Chris Hamilton, is almost all that remains to remind Oldham fans of the existence of one of the oldest and most famous rugby stadiums in the world. Built by a group of enthusiasts way back in 1889 it was condemned to death in 1996, linked to unfulfilled promises of a new stadium made by the local authority. The site of the old stadium is now a housing development, perhaps the saving grace being that the streets within the new estate are named in honour of past club players and officials.

Opposite: Scott Ranson brings down the curtain on Super League One when he scores the third of his hat-trick of tries against Sheffield Eagles.

Above: The 1997 squad that started Super League Two. From left to right, back row: Howard Hill, Brett Goldspink, Paul Atcheson, Ian Gildart, Vince Fawcett, Paul Davidson, Gary Lord, Rob Myler, Paul Topping, Jimmy Cowan. Middle row: Brian Gartland (second-team coach), Alan McCurrie (assistant coach), David Bradbury, Jason Temu, Mike Neal, David Stephenson, Afi Leuila, Joe Faimalo, Paul Crook, Nathan Turner, Nick Hodgson (physio), John Watkins (physio). Front row: Matt Munro, Darren Abram, Francis Maloney, Andy Goodway (coach), Martin Crompton (captain), Jim Quinn (chairman), Scott Ranson, John Clarke, Chris McKinney.

Opposite, above: To supplement Super League Two the 1997 World Club Championship was staged here and in France, as well as in Australia and New Zealand. It was competed for by the twelve clubs that made up European Super League and ten from Australian Super League plus Auckland Warriors. Oldham Bears were grouped with North Queensland Cowboys and Adelaide Rams in the qualifying stages. While well-beaten 54-16 by the Cowboys at the Stockland Stadium in Townsville and 42-14 by the Rams on the famous Adelaide Oval, the Bears were one of only a handful of European sides that won a match during the tournament, gaining revenge on the Cowboys with a 20-16 win at Boundary Park. Despite the euphoria only a paltry 2,900 fans turned up the following week for the home match against the Rams. Brisbane Broncos, who beat Hunter Mariners 36-12 in the final, lifted the trophy.

Opposite, below: The bookies had made the Bears favourites to finish bottom of Super League Two, despite finishing in a creditable eighth position the previous season. However, they rarely get it wrong and that's exactly where the Bears finished. Despite Paris St Germain disbanding, the Bears were still relegated. The financial storm clouds had gathered over the Oldham club for a number of years and despite the best endeavours of the directors the 121-year-old club was placed in the hands of the receiver and liquidated.

The announcement of the formation of a new club, Oldham RLFC (1997) Ltd, was broken to the press at Boundary Park in the autumn of 1997. The side would play the 1998 season in Division Two (two divisions below Super League) without a share of the News Corporation sponsorship, play its home matches at Boundary Park and promote once again the club's historic nickname the 'Roughyeds'. Pictured, from left to right, are Andrew Poxen (advisor), Melvyn Lord (club vice-chairman), Chris Hamilton (chairman), Brian Walker (consortium) and John Battye (leader of the council).

The team and coaching staff gathered to kick-off the 1998 season. From left to right, back row: Micky Edwards, Chris Eckersley, Brian Quinlan, Nathan Varley, Paul Round, Graeme Shaw, Keith Atkinson, Craig Diggle, Sean Cooper. Middle row: Paddy Kirwan (coach), Darren Robinson, Craig Barker, Richard Darkes, Jason Clegg, Martin Maders, Andrew Fleming, Afi Leuila, Steve Wanless (physio), Mick Coates (assistant coach). Front row: Mike Prescott, Steven Wilde, Neil Flanagan, John Hough, Ian Sinfield, Adrian Meade, Joe McNicholas.

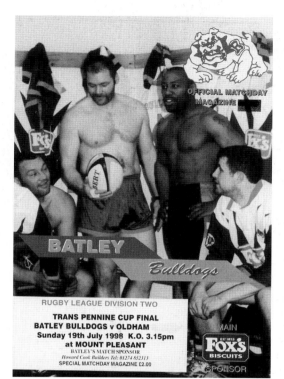

Right: During its first season the new club reached the final of the Trans-Pennine Cup, a competition devised to accommodate the eight clubs in Division Two. Oldham won the Lancashire side of the tournament but lost to the Yorkshire table-toppers, Batley Bulldogs, 28-12.

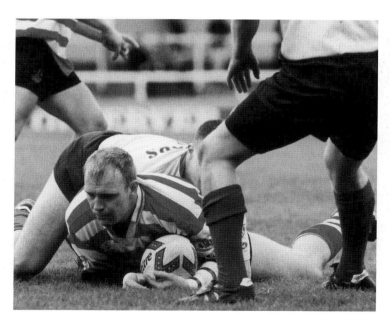

Second-row forward Graeme Shaw became the first player from the new club to gain international recognition when he was selected for the Scotland squad to compete in the Tri-Nations Championship of 1998. With Shaw as a substitute for both of their matches, Scotland lost 26-22 to France in Perpignan and 17-10 to Ireland on Partick Thistle's football ground.

The Roughyeds ended the 1998 season in fifth position out of a Division Two of eight clubs but the following season's campaign was a disaster. It was announced that all eighteen clubs outside of Super League would compete in just one division, to be known as the Northern Ford Premiership, but it was obvious from the kick-off that the strength of the Oldham squad was nowhere near the standard required and despite the best efforts of the beleaguered coaching staff, it ended the season next to bottom of the pile. The following season, Oldham-born scrum-half Mike Ford (above) was appointed player-coach and allowed to strengthen the squad sufficiently well to enable it to achieve sixth position and with it a place in the play-offs. The Ford-led side beat both Hull KR and Doncaster Dragons in the knock-out stages before going down 18-10 to Leigh Centurions in an exciting major semi-final.

By Easter of 2001 the Roughyeds didn't look like making the top-eight play-offs, never mind the Grand Final, but they picked themselves up by their bootlaces to win eleven consecutive matches to take fourth spot. Leigh Centurions and Rochdale Hornets were both beaten away from home to claim a place in the final against Widnes Vikings. On the day the Vikings proved the better of the two sides and, despite tries from Keith Brennan, Mike Ford and Kevin Mannion, plus a single goal from Pat Rich, the Vikings took their place in Super League, winning 24-14 in front of an 8,974 Spotland Stadium crowd.

The Oldham squad, September 2001. From left to right, back row: John Henderson (assistant coach), Kevin O' Loughlin, Dean Cross, Phil Farrell, Lee Doran, Chris Naylor, Ian Sinfield, Jason Clegg, Mark Sibson, Paul Norton, Anthony Gibbons, Danny Arnold, Tony O'Brien (conditioner). Middle row: Danni Turner (physio), Keith Brennan, Neil Roden, Chris Farrell, Kevin Mannion, Pat Rich, Danny Guest, Joe McNicholas, Warren Barrow, Leo Casey, Gavin Dodd, Lisa Sharrett (physio). Front row: Mark Knight (academy coach), Daryl Lacey, Gareth Barber, Joey Hayes, Andy Proctor, Mike Ford (player-coach), David Gibbons, James Wilkinson, Alex Peet, John Hough, Haydn Walker (second-team coach).

The 2002 season was hardly underway when player-coach Mike Ford announced that he was leaving the club to take up a coaching position with the Irish union international side and was quickly replaced by Australian John Harbin. There followed a devastating announcement that the club could not agree a satisfactory deal with landlords Oldham Athletic FC, being forced to leave Boundary Park to play its home matches out of town at Hurst Cross, the ground of Ashton United FC. Harbin didn't stay long either, taking up a coaching position with Oldham Athletic! In turn, he was replaced by Oldham-born ex-England prop Steve Molloy. Oldham squeezed into the play-offs, edging out Dewsbury Rams to take eighth position, but after disposing of Hull KR and Rochdale Hornets they lost to Batley Bulldogs in the minor semi-final.

Left: Two divisions outside Super League were reintroduced for season 2003, Oldham playing in the First Division at Boundary Park. The team won just 7 and drew 2 of an 18-match programme but still managed to take fifth spot and with it a place in the play-offs, losing to Hull KR at Craven Park in the elimination match. The cartoon drawing is of hooker John Hough and prop forward Jason Clegg.

Below: The Roughyeds beat Rochdale Hornets in a closely contested encounter to claim the 2004 A.J. Law Cup. Man of the match Ian Watson, Oldham's scrum half, is seen here being presented with the Heritage Trust Trophy by trustee Brian Walker. The Steve Molloy coached side finished fourth in National League One, its highest position since reforming in 1997, but lost out to Featherstone Rovers in the play-offs. Winger Nick Johnson scored 25 tries, the highest haul from an Oldham player for fourteen years.

Oldham faced the 2005 campaign with ex-New Zealand international Gary Mercer (photo) at the helm. The club experienced a dramatic exodus of players during the close season but strengthened with signings that included ex-Great Britain forward Simon Haughton, twice Challenge Cup finalist packman Ricky Bibey, ex Oldham Bear front-row forward Paul Norman, local born threequaters Alex Wilkinson and Damian Munro, Kiwi scrum-half Marti Turner and Tere Glassie, Dana Wilson and Carlos Matoera, a trio of players brought in from the Cook islands. Alas, the season started badly, the side were eliminated during the qualifying stanza of the Northern Rails Cup and subsequently failed to secure a win in their first four LHF Healthplan league matches. As though to prove things could still get worse the club announced that it had hit the financial buffers. But...

The club's hall of fame. From left to right: Alan Davies (1950-62), Bob Irving (1964-74), Andy Goodway (1979-85 and 1993-94), Derek Turner (1955-59), Bernard Ganley (1950-61), Martin Murphy (1966-82), Frank Stirrup (1950-62), John Etty (1954-59), Herman Hilton (1913-26) and Joe Ferguson (1899-23).

Other titles published by Tempus

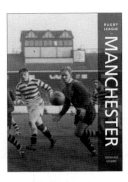

Rugby League in Manchester
GRAHAM MORRIS

Over the past century, senior rugby league has had a strong presence in Manchester, with no fewer than eleven venues staging the sport within a four-mile radius of the city centre. This unique publication, compiled by rugby league historian Graham Morris retraces the roots of Manchester's rugby league heritage, with the help of over 200 photographs and illustration, and is a fascinating reminder of the many great rugby league moments and matches that have taken place in Manchester over the last century.

0 7524 3087 4

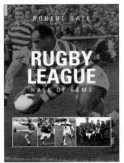

Rugby League Hall of Fame
ROBERT GATE

The Rugby League Hall of Fame was established in 1988 to celebrate the playing legends that have lit up the sport over the decades. This book celebrates these mighty heroes of the game and features a detailed personal and playing biography for each of them.

0 7524 2693 1

Bradford Rugby League
Bradford, Northern and Bulls
ROBERT GATE

Through their incarnations as Bradford, Northern or Bulls, the Bradford Rugby League club has been one of the most famous names in the history of the sport. This book illustrates their long and proud history with over 200 photographs and illustrations, many of which have never been published. With detailed captions from distinguished rugby league historian Robert Gate, this book is an essential read

0 7524 1896 3

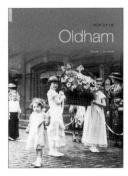

Voices of Oldham
DEREK SOUTHALL

Once the largest cotton-spinning centre in the world, Oldham was a vibrant town although many lived in poverty. The sense of community was very strong and this book records the stories and reminiscences of over thirty Oldhamers, in their own words. Their vivid voices recall childhood games, work, shops and entertainment, as well as the effects of war and bombing raids.

0 7524 3544 2

If you are interested in purchasing other books published by Tempus, or in case you have difficulty finding any Tempus books in your local bookshop, you can also place orders directly through our website

www.tempus-publishing.com